TEACHING Young Children

Second Edition

When I was a beginning preschool teacher in the 1970s, I was filled with eager enthusiasm and a strong desire to do a good job, but I didn't understand exactly what that meant. I volunteered on my church child care board, visited preschool classrooms in schools that had good reputations, and happily stumbled upon St. Andrew's United Methodist Weekday School in San Antonio, Texas.

The director of the school, Mrs. Eleanor Carnes, took me under her wing, nurtured my professional growth and development, and guided my steps in becoming an effective teacher of young children. She did that not only for me but for all of her teachers. Through the years, many new teachers who started their careers at St. Andrew's moved on to become early childhood program directors, college professors, and leaders in the field of early childhood education. None of us could have achieved the things we have achieved without the guidance and support that we received from our mentor and friend, Mrs. Eleanor Carnes.

So, Eleanor, this book is dedicated to you. I only hope that this book can do for another beginning teacher a little bit of what you did for me. Thank you for the inspiration!

Dianne Miller Nielsen

TEACHING Young Children

A Guide to Planning Your Curriculum,
Teaching Through Learning Centers,
and Just About Everything Else

Second Edition

Preschool–K

CORWIN PRESS
A SAGE Publications Company
Thousand Oaks, California

For information:

Corwin Press
A Sage Publications Company
2455 Teller Road
Thousand Oaks, California 91320
www.corwinpress.com

Sage Publications Ltd.
1 Oliver's Yard
55 City Road
London EC1Y 1SP
United Kingdom

Sage Publications India Pvt. Ltd.
B-42, Panchsheel Enclave
Post Box 4109
New Delhi 110 017 India

Printed in the United States of America.

Library of Congress Cataloging-in-Publication Data

Nielsen, Dianne Miller.
Teaching young children, Preschool-K : a guide to planning your curriculum, teaching through learning centers, and just about everything else / Dianne Miller Nielsen.— 2nd ed.
    p. cm.
Includes bibliographical references and index.
ISBN 1-4129-2672-6 (cloth) — ISBN 1-4129-2673-4 (pbk.)
    1. Early childhood education—United States. 2. Curriculum planning—United States. 3. Early childhood teachers—In-service training—United States. I. Title.
LB1139.25.N53 2006
372.21—dc22

2005037829

This book is printed on acid-free paper.

06   07   08   09   10   10   9   8   7   6   5   4   3   2   1

Acquisitions Editor:	Stacy Wagner
Production Editor:	Jenn Reese
Copy Editor:	Marjorie Cappellari
Typesetter:	C&M Digitals (P) Ltd.
Proofreader:	Dennis Webb
Indexer:	Karen McKenzie
Photography:	Terry Nielsen
Graphic Designer:	Lisa Miller

Contents

Preface

Classrooms for three- to six-year-olds can be found in public schools, private schools, Head Start programs, and child development centers in nearly every neighborhood in communities around the world. Some children attend part-day classes each morning, while others are in programs just a few mornings a week. Some programs offer full-day services, and still others provide evening and weekend care.

Regardless of these differences, however, high quality classrooms for young children share similar characteristics:

- Teachers with respect for and consideration of children's individuality
- Materials and activities that are age appropriate and developmentally appropriate
- An environment that reflects diversity in terms of home languages, cultures, and abilities

Preschool and kindergarten classrooms are very special places that provide just the right mix of what the children need in order to learn, grow, and develop—all in their own time and in their own way.

However, many excellent, experienced teachers find themselves bewildered when assigned to teach this age group, especially if their professional preparation was focused on teaching in the elementary grades. While they may recognize children's unique learning styles and special needs, they may not know how to handle a healthy amount of noise, activity, and even mess in their classroom! The ability to maintain control while allowing children to move about freely, or even sing, is likely something that teacher education classes didn't cover. Teachers who are new to the field may also feel overwhelmed: not sure where to begin in creating a classroom that is truly going to work for them and their children.

In the pages that follow, I will share with you the knowledge I have gained from my 30-plus years of experience as a classroom teacher, administrator, and teacher trainer in many different types of early childhood settings. As a long-time member of the National Association for the Education of Young Children, I am a staunch supporter of the principles of developmentally appropriate practice as defined and described by that organization. I have endeavored, in this book, to help make those principles concrete and attainable for you, the early childhood professional.

What This Book Offers

The book explores the reasons behind the things we do in effective early childhood classrooms, some of the common educational goals and objectives for 3–6 year olds, and what the teacher's role is in a classroom that is based on hands-on exploration and learning through doing. How to write lesson plans, how to develop your daily schedule, how to arrange your furniture and equipment, and how to manage your daily activities and routines are also addressed in these pages. Throughout the book, you will find a treasure trove of helpful hints and tips, including ideas for ways to enhance the children's learning through modeling, interactions, and conversations. The first edition of *Teaching Young Children* has been referred to as a "cookbook" for teaching preschool and kindergarten. It was written to make teachers feel comfortable and confident as they went about helping children learn, grow, and develop their skills and knowledge.

New to This Edition

This second edition of *Teaching Young Children* is designed with the same goals in mind as the first edition, but it has been updated and expanded in light of our changing world and changes in educational legislation. New elements include

- A chapter on setting up and managing an ABC center to further aid with literacy skill development
- A chapter on setting up and managing a computer center, both to bring new technology into the classroom and to extend literacy activities to the computer
- A chapter on involving parents and families inside and outside of the classroom
- Sidebar tips for teachers throughout the chapters, from activities and ideas to experiment with ("Try This") to important concepts to remember ("Keep in Mind").

A chapter on field trips in the first edition has been extended to address other special events, such as visitors to the classroom. The Resources section at the end of the book has been significantly expanded as well. All other chapters have been updated in relevant places to meet the needs of the contemporary early childhood educator.

Use this book as your guide as you begin preparing your own wonderful learning environment, and get ready to enjoy an exciting, challenging, and rewarding adventure as a teacher of young children!

Acknowledgments

Few good works are accomplished by an individual alone. Such is the case with the creation of this book. I am grateful to the help, support, and encouragement from so many colleagues who contributed to this edition of *Teaching Young Children*. I am especially thankful for . . .

. . . My best friend, business partner, and husband, Terry Nielsen, for providing suggestions, editing first drafts, and taking the wonderful photos that grace the pages of this book. What would I do without you?

. . . Frank Guevara and his excellent staff at Palo Alto College Ray Ellison Family Center, San Antonio, Texas.

. . . Elisa Romansanta and her outstanding staff at DePaul Family Center, San Antonio, Texas, for allowing us to use their centers for photographs.

. . . Terry Brown and her talented preschool staff at On Board Software Family Center, a Bright Horizons Family Solutions program in San Antonio, Texas, for the beautiful classroom seen on the cover of the book.

. . . And last, but certainly not least, to my early childhood education students, past and present, who have helped me understand the needs of emerging teachers of young children and have taught me how to help them achieve excellence.

Corwin Press gratefully acknowledges the insight and guidance of the following reviewers:

Larry Garf, Instructor, Pacific Oaks College, Pasadena, CA
Sheri Green, former kindergarten teacher, Muncie, IN
Kim Keeter, Past President, San Antonio Association for the Education of Young Children, San Antonio, TX
Deborah Nuzzi, Principal, Robert Frost School, Bournbonnais, IL

About the Author

Dianne Miller Nielsen has been an early childhood educator for more than 30 years. She currently owns an early childhood teacher training agency, Nielsen Training Services, Inc. This agency provides workshops, seminars, and courses for early childhood teachers and child care center directors, including training for the nationally recognized Child Development Associate (CDA) credential. She is currently designated as a Master Trainer in the Texas Early Care and Education Trainer Registry. Dianne is also an active member of the National Association for the Education of Young Children, contributing to the journal *Young Children* and continuing to serve as a validator for program accreditation. She recently completed her second term as vice-president of the San Antonio chapter of NAEYC. Dianne is a speaker, often delivering keynote addresses, at many national, state, and local conferences. In November 2005, Dianne was presented with a Congressional Award for distinguished and outstanding service and dedication to the community, the state, and the nation.

Through the years Dianne has worked in nearly every facet of early childhood education. She has been a public school teacher at the Pre-K through first-grade levels, a distance learning teacher for Pre-K through third-grade levels, a preschool and kindergarten classroom teacher, and a child care center director in the private nonprofit sector, as well as the education specialist for a multisite Head Start program. She served as the deputy administrator of a very large child development program on a military installation in California and as adjunct faculty in the child development department of San Antonio College. She currently provides consultation services for a number of early childhood programs.

As a writer, Dianne has revised many of Clare Cherry's beloved books (*Creative Art for the Developing Child, Creative Movement for the Developing Child,* and *Please Don't Sit on the Kids*), and has authored several of her own books, including the first edition of the book you now hold in your hands, *Opening the Classroom Window*, and *Preschool Multiple Intelligences*.

Dianne and her husband, Terry Nielsen, live in South Texas where they breed Appaloosa and Foundation Quarter horses, operate an international equine transport business, and publish *Texas Horse News*, a monthly magazine for equine enthusiasts.

Welcome to the Early Childhood Profession!

Young children have special needs, varied learning styles, and boundless energy! So, as you might imagine, a classroom for young children is a very special place. An effective preschool or kindergarten classroom is a unique, exciting, interesting place where active learning happens from the minute the first child walks through the door. This classroom will look, sound, and feel very different from those designed to meet the needs of older children. In a classroom for young children, learning is characterized by purposeful noise, activity, and a certain amount of mess. Children will be moving about freely—talking, singing, laughing, and learning together. There are no worksheets or workbooks in sight. There are no desks and no formal reading groups.

Programs for young children have various names. They are called "early childhood," "preschool," "Head Start," "Pre-K," and "kindergarten." The facilities that provide these programs may be called "child development center," "child care center," "early childhood center," or "school." Funding may come from the government, or they may be privately owned and operated businesses. Some children attend part-day classes each morning while others participate in a two or three mornings a week program. Some facilities are open for longer hours, offering care and education from 6 A.M. until 6 P.M. every day of the work week. Some programs provide evening and weekend care.

Regardless of these differences, however, high-quality classrooms for young children share similar characteristics. In every type of program, children's individuality is respected and considered. An early childhood classroom is a place filled with age-appropriate activities, schedules, and routines. Diversity in terms of home languages, cultures, and abilities is reflected in the environment. Early childhood classrooms are very special places that provide just the right mix of what the children need in order to learn, grow, and develop—all in their own time and in their own way.

It is my hope that this book will serve as your guide as you begin preparing your own wonderful learning environment for the young children in your care. Get ready for an exciting, challenging, and rewarding adventure as a teacher of young children.

Best Wishes!
Dianne Miller Nielsen

Part I

Early Childhood Education Goals, Roles, and Curriculum Planning

Back in the eighteenth century, the philosopher Jean-Jacques Rousseau proposed the idea that there was something special and unique about the way young children think and learn. He believed that young children were not just miniature adults but had their own style and needs. This notion was not initially accepted, but over time more and more people came to believe that Rousseau was correct.

In the 1860s, a German educator named Frederick Froebel established the first "kindergarten." Literally translated, the word kindergarten means "children's garden." Froebel agreed with Rousseau that young children are unique, and he believed that they needed a special environment for learning. He hoped to provide them with a "garden" in which they might develop through careful nurturing. As a result of his beliefs, Froebel's kindergarten was very different from other schools that existed at the time. His kindergarten was an active place where children were involved in many hands-on, real-life experiences. The children began learning through their play. Froebel believed so much in the value of play in early childhood education that he called it the "highest expression of human development."

As time went by, more and more educators began looking into what Froebel had accomplished. Schools for young children began to spring up all over the world. By the 1920s, nursery schools and kindergartens were firmly established in the United States as well as in other countries. Patty Smith Hill was a pioneer in this field in the United States during this time period. Maria Montessori, founder of the now-popular Montessori Method, established a school for young children in Italy during the first decade of the twentieth century. Early childhood education was definitely catching on!

In the 1960s, the United States government recognized the importance of early childhood education and established Head Start programs. The goal of Head Start then—as now—was to provide the advantage of high-quality early childhood education to children from low-income families. The program is based on the belief that the early years are crucial and that a good early childhood education gives children a solid foundation on which to build future educational efforts. Head Start continues to make a positive difference in the lives of many young children throughout the nation.

Another project that began in the 1960s was the Perry Preschool Project in Ypsilanti, Michigan. The Perry Preschool Project took a long-range look at children from low-income families who attended a quality preschool. The researchers followed the children throughout their school years to see if their preschool experiences made a positive difference in their lives. The results were amazing. Overall, the children who had been in the early childhood program were successful throughout their school years. They stayed in school until graduation, stayed out of trouble with the law, and went on to become productive, successful citizens. The Perry Preschool Project proved that money spent on education for young children seemed to pay off by producing adults who made positive contributions to society.

In the 1980s, when the Perry Preschool Project children were becoming young adults, lawmakers throughout the United States began to take notice of the results. So many children were dropping out of school and turning to drugs and crime that the idea of a special program to get children off to a good start was exciting. States began introducing legislation to establish prekindergarten programs for certain three- and four-year-olds in the public schools. Public schools also began providing special education programs for preschoolers with various disabilities.

Today, universal preschool is a concept that is gaining momentum. In some states, every child is eligible for publicly funded preschool, regardless of family income or other risk factors. Today, every preschool-age child with a diagnosed disability is eligible for public school services, often in a system of total inclusion within the prekindergarten classrooms. Today, most preschool-age children in the United States who are "at-risk" in terms of income or whose home languages are not English are eligible for free, publicly-funded prekindergarten education.

Early childhood educators are facing an exciting and challenging future. We now have solid, research-based information available to us that was previously unknown (Bredekamp & Copple, 1997; Burns, Snow, & Griffin, 1998). Current technological breakthroughs have enabled neuroscientists to unravel many of the mysteries about the development of the human brain. Research has shown that the three-year-old child's brain is twice as active, connected, and flexible as the adult brain (Shore, 1997). Science has also proven that the quality of a young child's experiences and environment quite literally shape the child's brain, causing connections between brain cells to form and strengthen. Human brain development is truly driven by experience.

Given this research-based knowledge, we understand now that the quality of a young child's experiences and environment play an extremely critical role in the child's future. And we know now that those of us who interact with young children quite literally hold the future in our hands.

Unfortunately, some programs for young children have been established hastily, without adequate understanding of the special nature of early childhood education. It is up to us, as teachers of young children, to ensure that our classrooms and our curricula are developmentally appropriate and that the early years are a special and wonderful time for each and every child whose lives we touch.

1

Goals of Early Childhood Education

Recent research supports the notion that planned, purposeful, and productive play is the most important part of the learning environment for young children. Children must explore, experiment, and make discoveries for themselves through playful interactions with the environment and with other people in order to make sense of their world.

Children need many interesting things to touch, taste, hear, smell, and see. In a high-quality, developmentally-appropriate preschool or kindergarten environment, children will be painting, dressing up, playing house, building with blocks, working with puzzles, looking at colorful picture books, digging in sand, pouring water, riding tricycles, beating drums, watering plants, feeding guinea pigs, dancing, pretending, and much, much more.

Exploration and Discovery Through Play

The major goal of the early childhood classroom is to expose children to wonderful things to explore and discover through their self-directed play. While it may be an accomplishment for children of this age to be able to recite the alphabet or count to 100, it is far more important to support their natural curiosity and desire to learn by giving them rich and meaningful learning opportunities that are relevant to them—their lives, their families, their cultures, their languages, and their special abilities and needs.

Teaching to Multiple Intelligences

We must also consider the groundbreaking work done by Dr. Howard Gardner, the Harvard professor who developed the theory of multiple intelligences. Thanks to Dr. Gardner's insights, we now understand that human beings have at least eight different ways of expressing intelligence—and that these intelligences must be considered when planning learning experiences for children in order to ensure that every child's needs will be met. Therefore, good early childhood classrooms are filled with opportunities for children to use language, logical thinking, music, art, nature, movement, interactions with others, and solitary endeavors.

Meeting Developmental Needs

As a teacher of young children, it is important to help individuals in your classroom reach their full potential. In doing that, you must watch for signs of growth in many different developmental domains—language, physical, social, emotional, and cognitive. Specific goals and objectives for young children will vary from school to school, age group to age group, and culture to culture. There are some broad goals, however, that are shared by many early childhood educators and are thus reflected in most early childhood programs. Here are a few sample goals that are common to many early childhood programs.

Oral Language Development

Oral language development is generally divided into two separate areas—expressive language and receptive language. Before children can learn to read and write, they must be able to speak and listen effectively. Phonological awareness—the ability to recognize sounds of language—is essential in this domain of development.

Goals for *expressive* oral language development:

1. Communicates nonverbally through gestures, movements, and expressions
2. Uses language to express needs, ideas, feelings, common routines, and familiar scripts
3. Participates in informal conversations about experiences and follows conversational rules
4. Begins to identify rhymes and rhyming sounds in familiar words, participates in rhyming games, and repeats rhyming songs and poems
5. Begins to retell the sequence of stories
6. Uses terms related to direction and position (up, down, top, bottom, on, off, over, under)
7. Begins to attend to the beginning sounds in familiar words by identifying that the pronunciations of several words all begin the same way
8. Begins to break words into syllables, or claps along with each syllable in a phrase
9. Begins to create and invent words by substituting one sound for another
10. Shows a steady increase in speaking vocabulary

Goals for *receptive* oral language development:

1. Responds appropriately to simple questions
2. Identifies and compares familiar sounds (animals, machines, family members' voices)
3. Becomes aware of repetitive patterns in rhymes, chants, and poetry
4. Recalls facts, details, and sequence of events in stories
5. Recognizes variations in vocal tones to express emotion
6. Focuses attention on a speaker
7. Understands and follows simple oral directions
8. Enjoys listening to and responding to books
9. Listens to and engages in several exchanges of conversation with others
10. Listens to recorded stories and music and shows understanding through gestures, actions, and/or language

Literacy Development

Literacy skills begin developing at a very early age, as a natural outgrowth of oral language skill development. Typically, developing children who are in environments that are print-rich and that provide many meaningful opportunities for reading and writing develop literacy skills almost as easily as they develop oral language skills. All young children, regardless of developmental levels, delays, or challenges, benefit from being in a print-rich environment that is filled with appropriate literacy experiences.

Goals for literacy development:

1. Demonstrates an interest in books, attempting to read and write independently

2. Uses known letters and approximations of letters to represent written language

3. Understands that reading and writing are ways to obtain information and knowledge; generates and communicates thoughts and ideas and solves problems

4. Begins to dictate words, phrases, and sentences to an adult who is recording on paper

5. Identifies at least ten letters of the alphabet (PreK); identifies all letters of the alphabet (Kindergarten)

6. Associates sounds with written words

7. Understands that print carries a message by recognizing labels, signs, and other print forms in the environment

8. Begins to understand some basic print conventions

9. Begins to make some letter/sound matches (PreK); able to make most letter/sound matches (Kindergarten)

10. Begins to identify some high-frequency words

Cognitive Development

Cognitive development includes the development of thinking skills such as identifying, classifying, comparing, contrasting, sequencing, predicting, and problem solving.

Goals for cognitive development:

❶ Matches objects in a one-to-one correspondence

❷ Identifies numbers of objects (0–10) in a group

❸ Uses the senses as a way to gain information and compare objects

❹ Describes events and objects in the environment

❺ Sorts objects according to various characteristics (color, shape, size)

❻ Uses vocabulary to compare quantity (more, less) and size (bigger, smaller)

❼ Demonstrates awareness of part-whole relationships through puzzles

❽ Repeats a simple pattern with beads, blocks, or other objects

❾ Orders a limited amount of objects by size

❿ Recalls the sequence of events in a familiar story, classroom activity, or daily routine

Physical Development

Physical development is just as important as language and thinking skills and is a vital part of early childhood education. Physical development can be broken down into three areas. *Gross motor development* is the development of the large muscles in the body. *Fine motor development* focuses on the small muscles in the fingers and hands. *Sensory development* supports children's development of their five senses.

Goals for Physical Development:

❶ Develops the ability to travel in different ways in a group without bumping into others or falling down

❷ Demonstrates clear contrasts between slow and fast movement

❸ Demonstrates non-locomotor movements such as bending and stretching

❹ Develops the ability to balance on one foot for increasing periods of time

❺ Practices self-help skills (buttoning, zipping)

❻ Develops eye-hand coordination

❼ Develops the ability to walk forward and sideways on a balance beam without falling

❽ Participates in active play, gaining skills related to the control of movements

❾ Develops the ability to toss and catch a ball

❿ Demonstrates increasing awareness of selected body parts, such as head, back, chest, waist, hips, arms, elbows, wrists, hands, fingers, legs, knees, ankles, feet, and toes

Aesthetic Development

It is important to expose young children to beauty and to help them develop an appreciation for fine art. For some children, artistic self-expression is the most natural way to communicate thoughts, feelings, and ideas while challenging their imaginations and developing the ability to think reflectively and to solve problems creatively.

Goals for aesthetic development:

❶ Explores line, color, shape, and texture through art activities

❷ Experiments with various art materials and tools

❸ Expresses ideas and feelings through art

❹ Develops awareness and appreciation of art culture

❺ Sings songs and listens to music

❻ Responds to music through body movements

❼ Explores various rhythm and melody instruments

❽ Dramatizes stories

❾ Uses body movements to express feelings and ideas

❿ Uses puppets to express feelings and ideas

Social and Emotional Development

A final area of concern for teachers of young children is the social and emotional development of their students. Self concept, self control, cooperation, social relationships, and knowledge of their families and communities are all elements of this developmental domain. Learning to identify, communicate, and manage their emotions effectively enables children to form friendships and gain social competence—one of the primary goals of a good early childhood program.

Goals for social and emotional development:

1. Develops growing capacity for independence and self-help skill development in a range of activities, routines, and tasks

2. Develops and expresses awareness of self in terms of gender, family composition, specific abilities, characteristics, and preferences

3. Shows pride in accomplishments

4. Demonstrates increasing abilities in expressing feelings, needs, and opinions in difficult situations and conflicts without harming themselves, others, or property

5. Demonstrates growing understanding of how their actions affect others and begins to accept the consequences of their actions

6. Demonstrates increasing comfort in talking with and accepting guidance and directions from a range of familiar adults

7. Progresses in responding sympathetically to peers who are in need, upset, hurt or angry, and in expressing empathy or caring for others

8. Progresses in understanding similarities and respecting differences among people, such as gender, race, special needs, culture, language, and family composition

9. Develops growing awareness of work and what is required to perform various tasks

10. Begins to express and understand concepts of geography in the contexts of home, classroom, and community

These goals are common to many programs for children aged three through six. Regardless of your setting, it is wise to develop goals such as these so that you and the parents of the children enrolled in your care have a common understanding of what you hope the child will achieve during the preschool and kindergarten years. A clearly stated set of goals will also help you in the lesson planning process, making planning purposeful and goal-oriented.

2

The Teacher's Role

Teaching in a preschool or kindergarten classroom is challenging. It is physically demanding because there is rarely a moment to sit down. It is mentally and emotionally demanding because it requires that you be constantly alert and always searching for ways to extend the children's discoveries and enhance their learning. Teaching young children can be more difficult and demanding than teaching older children! It is also tremendously rewarding when you see young children develop into independent and self-confident thinkers, doers, and problem-solvers.

The following is a list of roles that teachers of young children must assume in order to provide quality learning experiences. By fulfilling these roles, you will teach children to think independently and creatively, to ask questions and look for their own answers through experimenting and exploring, to become aware of their own uniqueness and to value themselves as worthwhile human beings, and to get along peacefully in the world with others.

Planner

Your first and most important job is to plan and prepare the environment for learning. Because young children learn through play, it is essential that you provide the materials and equipment necessary for meaningful play activities that support the development of multiple intelligences. The classroom and the outdoor area must be set up with care so that the children will find interesting, stimulating, meaningful, and challenging things to do in an atmosphere that is orderly, safe, and has a sense of purpose.

Young children also learn best when they feel emotionally safe and supported. When planning your classroom, always keep in mind the children's ethnicities, cultures, languages, and differing abilities. Make sure that your environment, including your books, music, posters, pictures, dolls, dramatic play props, cooking activities, and the overall tone of your interactions, reflects a respect and concern for each child as a unique individual and as a member of a family and a community.

In such a carefully planned learning environment, children will learn that school is a happy, safe, and interesting place in which they can explore, discover, and learn about themselves and the world around them. With this belief system in place they are prepared to move forward into the more structured world of "school" with eager anticipation and ready for success.

Facilitator

When the planning and preparation are finished and children arrive for the day, your role shifts to that of a facilitator. It is your job to make sure that every child has the opportunity to experience success and learn according to individual needs, styles, and levels of ability. Move about the classroom and the outdoor area while the children are playing. Watch, listen, and talk with the children during their play.

Ask open-ended questions to help children extend their thinking and stretch their vocabulary. Open-ended questions are those with many possible answers. Some examples of open-ended questions are:

- "What did you notice about the paint at the easel today?"
- "What do you think will happen when you put the cork in the water?"
- "Tell me about the lemon."

For additional questioning ideas, see Bloom's Taxonomy on page 23.

While moving about the learning environment, be alert for special moments of discovery—"teachable moments"—when a child is on the brink of learning something new. When this happens, move closer and help the child take the new ideas a step or two further. For example, two children have built towers with blocks and they notice that one tower is taller than the other. This is a good time to move in and begin talking with the children about ways in which the towers are the same and ways in which they are different. Suggest measuring the towers and encourage the children to think of ways to do the measuring. They might suggest using a piece of yarn, their hands, their feet, their shoes, a tape measure, or a yardstick. Encourage children to go from that point to measuring other objects in the room, comparing measurements, and "writing" their results on paper.

When you are working with children in this exploratory way, always remember that their learning will be less meaningful if you give them the answer or take over the direction of the activity. When you facilitate children's learning, you are setting things up and providing materials, time, space, and encouragement so that they can find their own answers in their own way and in their own time. That's what early learning is all about.

Observer

The children's playtime is also a time for you to observe each child carefully. Through careful observation of children at work and play you can begin to see which skills they have mastered and which skills need additional reinforcement. Your observations can give you insight into which intelligences are used more than others by a particular child. They may also raise your awareness of a child's cultural, linguistic, or developmental needs. These observations will help you plan for the next day or week.

If, for example, you see that a child has mastered all of the puzzles in the classroom, make a note of that and plan to provide more difficult puzzles the next day. If you notice that a child is calling all of the shapes in the block center "squares," make a note of that observation and plan to spend more time with that child, mentioning the names of shapes that are encountered throughout the classroom. When that child chooses a block activity, you might go into the block center and say, "I see you've used many triangles in your building today," as you point to the triangles. If that same child chooses to paint circles at the easel, say, "You're painting a circle." By casually mentioning the names of shapes over a period of days and weeks and months of play, the child is likely to learn the names of shapes easily and naturally.

Anecdotal Records

It is helpful to keep anecdotal records of observations like those mentioned above. Make a section in a recipe-card file box with each child's name on it. Write anecdotal notes and the date of the observation on index cards. Be specific. For example, a good notation would be, "Julia completed a ten-piece puzzle without assistance." With this notation, you know that Julia needs to be exposed to more difficult puzzles, and you can plan to provide those challenges in the days to come. Vague comments like, "Julia has good eye-hand coordination" are less helpful to you when you are planning new opportunities for the child. File the cards behind the child's name in the file box.

Portfolio

Add these observations to a collection of children's work, developmental checklists, and parent observations and you have a good overview of the child's strengths, needs, and interests. Many teachers put such collections together into a box or set of folders called a "portfolio." Portfolios are used for assessment and for planning, and they enable the teacher to provide an individually appropriate experience for each child.

Model

Social skills such as cooperating, getting along with others, and communicating effectively to solve problems can be modeled through actions and words. You will be teaching politeness and courtesy when you say "please" and "thank you" to the children and to other adults in the room. When you look at your lesson plans or read a note from a parent, you are modeling the importance of reading and writing. When you wipe up a spill or help put the blocks back on the shelf at clean-up time, you are showing by example that taking care of the classroom and keeping it neat and orderly are important things to do. When you're feeling upset or angry, you can teach children how to deal with strong emotions by expressing your feelings in a socially acceptable way. Modeling is a very powerful teaching technique. It's amazing how quickly you will begin hearing your own words and seeing your own actions reflected in the children's behavior.

Modeling During Play

Another way to serve as a model for children is by entering into their play. The reasons for entering into their play are to help them get started with new or unfamiliar materials or to help them through difficult social experiences. If, for example, there is a new game and the children don't understand how it works, play the game with the children until they are able to do it themselves. As soon as you think they can handle it without you, move on and encourage them to continue independently. If you see that a child is standing off to the side of the dramatic play center, feeling unsure about how to participate with others, join in the play and pretend to be a neighbor who has come for tea. Sit down at the table and invite the reluctant child to serve you tea. As soon as you see that the newcomer has been accepted into the play environment, step out of the situation and encourage the children's play to progress.

Keep in Mind

It is important to remember to enter into the play for only as long as you are needed. You are not there to "call the shots" or direct the play activity. As soon as you see that the children are able to take charge, step away and move on.

Support System

Children need the safety and security of knowing that you will be there for them when they need you. There will be times when an adult's assistance is truly needed—opening a sticky glue bottle, getting a drippy painting to the drying rack, getting a CD or computer game started, unfastening tight buttons for a quick trip to the toilet, or providing hugs and comfort for a child who has fallen down or bumped an elbow.

At the same time, you must be constantly alert to ways to support the children's emerging self-help skills. Encourage children to help each other. For example, if a child asks for help putting on a paint smock, do not quickly put it on for him or her. Instead, encourage the child to try it independently. If, after trying alone, the child still needs help, suggest that he or she ask a friend for help. This accomplishes several goals:

❶ It encourages children to be helpful and nurturing toward one another.

❷ It frees you from the task of putting on and taking off smocks throughout the day.

❸ Children learn a lot from each other, and oftentimes peer instruction is the most effective form of teaching

The same rule applies to all sorts of self-help situations, like buttoning and zipping jackets, wiping up spills, hanging up sweaters, and putting on shoes. Don't be too quick to come to a child's rescue. Helping too quickly denies children the opportunity to learn to solve problems for themselves. Children who never take care of their own needs often feel helpless and powerless. Build up children's feelings of self-worth and self-confidence by enabling them to accomplish simple tasks such as buttoning their own sweater independently.

Provide Scaffolding

Another way early childhood teachers support children is by providing "scaffolding" for learning. Just as a new building under construction requires scaffolding to support its progress, young children benefit from having an adult or an older, more experienced child support their progress in making sense of the world around them, helping them accomplish tasks that are too difficult for them to do alone. The primary ingredient in providing scaffolding is you! When children are engaged in play throughout the room, stay tuned in to their needs. Watch for "teachable moments," and be ready to help children develop new skills that build on existing skills. For example, if a child is having difficulty working a puzzle, you might sit with the child and talk about the shapes of the pieces, helping them match curved lines to curved lines and parts of pictures to related parts. Talk them through the activity and support their emerging skills and knowledge.

Team Player

Whether your title is "teacher," "assistant," "aide," or "caregiver," there's a good chance that you will share your classroom with other staff members. Many classrooms for young children have at least two adults and often more, depending on the number of children. Each staff member is an important part of the teaching team. In the early childhood classroom, team members should work together very closely, joining forces to facilitate learning for the children. As with any type of team, each member has specific responsibilities. It is important that each team member's responsibilities are clearly understood by all so that the classroom can function smoothly and effectively.

Teachers

Typically, the teacher is the staff member who has special training in Child Development or Early Childhood Education and is held accountable for the children's educational experiences. Because of this special training and accountability, it is the teacher's job to plan and implement the curriculum, implement classroom management techniques, assess children's growth and development, make referrals for special needs, and report progress to parents. While most teachers welcome suggestions from other caregivers, the final decision in all matters related to the children's education lies in the teacher's hands.

Teaching Assistants

Other caregivers, such as assistants or aides, are typically responsible for helping the teacher manage the classroom and implement the curriculum. Division of specific duties will vary from classroom to classroom and should be decided upon by each teaching team. Team members should sit down together at the beginning of the school year and talk about how they will divide the responsibilities.

Because each teacher has his or her own style, it is usually a good idea for an assistant to begin the school year by observing the teacher. This will help the assistant get a feel for the teacher's methods. When the assistant is uncertain about something the teacher does or expects, it's important to ask questions and come to a mutual understanding of what is expected of him/her.

Effective Communication

The adults in the classroom must communicate with each other daily, especially before and after school. When the children are in the classroom, there is no time to engage in lengthy discussions about teaching practices or philosophies. During class time, all members of the teaching team need to devote their full attention to the task at hand—facilitating the children's learning. Therefore, using a notebook system is an effective way to communicate with team members. Write down questions, ideas, and suggestions that come to mind throughout the day. At some point in the day, each team member should check the notebook to see if there are any messages or points for discussion. The notebook serves as an ongoing two-way communication system.

This is especially important in full-day programs that employ different morning and afternoon staff. Before the morning staff goes home for the day, vital information must be communicated to the afternoon staff. This is essential for continuity in the child's day and for smooth overall operation of the program. In addition to the "communications notebook" method, set aside a block of time once or twice a week for a team meeting. This special time gives each team member a chance to share ideas, questions, suggestions, and concerns. It's also a good time to visit with each other, get to know each other, and build healthy relationships.

Handling Conflict

As with every close relationship, conflicts and misunderstandings will arise from time to time. It happens in families, in friendships, in marriages, and in teaching teams. In order to prevent little problems and misunderstandings from getting out of control, each team member must share his or her concerns clearly and directly as soon as possible. Little things left unspoken can become big problems! Talk things out, face to face, with honesty and mutual respect. When all team members work at establishing and maintaining a healthy working relationship, their effectiveness in the classroom is strengthened and the school days are happy, productive times for everyone.

Questioner

Dr. Benjamin Bloom was a noted educator who contributed greatly to the field, especially in the area of cognitive development. He created a system to categorize thinking skills, known as Bloom's Taxonomy. As you ask children open-ended questions to extend their learning, ask questions from each category. You might even find it helpful to post a copy of the taxonomy at several of the learning centers to serve as a reminder.

Bloom's Taxonomy

Category	Sample Questions
Knowledge Recalling bits of information Children identify, name, define, describe, match, and select.	What is the name of _____ ? Where is the _____ ? What different kinds of _____ are there? What happened first? Next? Last?
Comprehension Understanding the meaning of the experience Children explain, classify, summarize, predict outcomes, and sort objects.	How are _____ and _____ alike? How are they different? Why do you think _____ happened? What might have caused _____? Tell me about _____ .
Application Using what was learned in a new situation Children solve problems, demonstrate discoveries, and modify and rearrange materials.	How else could you use _____? What would happen if _____? What would you use to _____? How would you make _____? What would you need in order to _____?
Analysis Breaking an idea or activity into separate components Children separate, order, subdivide, estimate, and infer.	How do you know this is a _____? In which group does this belong? Why? Is this a _____ or a _____? Why?
Synthesis Combining parts to make a whole Children combine, create, design, compose, construct, and rearrange.	Can you think of a new way to _____? Draw a picture about _____ . Tell me a story about _____ . How could you make _____? Pretend that you are a _____ .
Evaluation Making value judgments Children criticize, compare, justify, conclude, discriminate, and support.	Which do you like best? Why? What do you like about _____? Why? What don't you like about _____? Why? What is the best thing about _____? Why? What is the worst thing about _____? Why?

Adapted and developed by the author from a number of sources over a period of years. See, among other sources, Bloom, B. S. (1969). *Taxonomy of Educational Objectives: The Classification of Educational Goals.* United Kingdom: Longman Group.

3

Planning a Curriculum for Young Children

Before you make decisions about the physical arrangement of your classroom and daily schedules and routines, you must first make some decisions about what you want children to learn, accomplish, and experience. For planning purposes, however, it is wise to keep in mind as you plan that preschool learning environments are divided into clearly identified learning centers. There are seven basic centers that are the mainstay of many classrooms for young children. These centers are

Art

Blocks

Dramatic Play

Literacy (which may be one large center or several more focused ones, such as a listening center and puppet center to develop oral language skills, and a library center, writing center, ABC center, and computer center for reading and writing skills)

Math and Manipulatives

Music

Science

Many teachers choose to add one or more of the following centers to the basic seven:

Cooking

Woodworking

Clay and Dough

Construction

Sensory

Outdoor Play

Some learning centers can be a combination of several. How many centers you choose to have and how you combine the activities will depend on many factors: the space and materials you have available, the children's needs and interests, and your own personal preferences. A complete list of set-up suggestions, teaching tips, and management ideas for each of the centers listed above begins on page 35.

Emergent Curriculum

Curriculum for young children does not come from a resource book or a curriculum guide. While resource books and curriculum guides can be helpful, authentic early childhood curriculum comes from the children themselves. It is built around their interests, their needs, their developmental levels, and their unique personalities.

Curriculum also comes from you—your goals for the children, both as a group and as individuals; your observations of the children's skills, needs, and interests; and your own interests, culture, and unique personality. Curriculum for young children also comes from their families—their lifestyles, culture, preferred languages, values, and goals for their children. No two classrooms will have exactly the same curriculum because no two groups of children and teachers will be exactly alike. They will, no doubt, share some common goals and objectives, but they will each have their own unique flair.

Getting Started

So how do you get started planning curriculum? Observe and listen to the children as they play. What topics come up? What play themes do you see emerging? What materials or activities capture their interest? What questions do they ask you or each other?

Next, listen to their families. What do the families tell you about the children's interests, skills, and knowledge? What kinds of activities do the families enjoy doing together? What do the parents want their children to know more about? What are the cultural and linguistic influences that must be considered?

Finally, ask yourself if the topics that you see emerging among your children are "big enough" to delve into as a project or unit of study. Also, ask yourself if **you** find the topic interesting. Your enthusiastic interest in the topic is critical to the success of the project.

K-W-L Chart

When you've selected a topic, one way to begin writing your plans is to create a K-W-L chart with the children. "K-W-L" stands for what the students already "**k**now" about the topic, what the students "**w**ant" to know about the topic," and, at the end of the lesson, what students have "**l**earned" about the topic.

Sit down with a large sheet of chart paper and a marker. Make three columns on the paper. Label the first column "We Know." Label the second column "We Want to Know." Label the third column "We Learned." Ask the children what they know about the topic. Write their ideas in the first column. Next, move on to the "We Want to Know" column and ask for their questions about the topic. You may want to revisit this chart for several days.

Include Parents

When you have enough information from the children, it's time to go to the parents for help. Send a note home and/or put up a large sheet of chart paper on your parent bulletin board or in the hallway outside your classroom. Tell the parents about the project you are planning and ask them for ideas. Be sure to let them know that you would love for them to share any resources that they might have, including special talents or skills that they would be willing to demonstrate for the children.

Add Your Ideas

After you've gathered ideas from the children and the families, it's time for you to add your own ideas. Try to integrate the ideas throughout the classroom so that children who are building with blocks, children who are exploring science activities, and children who are looking at books are all experiencing the same concept in different ways. Plan for your whole classroom to fit together in a way that is logical and unified.

Teaching Through Projects

Teaching through projects gives you a framework for planning. For example, here are just a few activities children might participate in at each of the seven basic learning centers if your project is "Household Pets."

Art Center

Print with dog biscuits

Make fake fur collages

Glue feathers on tissue rolls

Make collages with shells and sand on heavy cardboard bases

Blocks Center

Add vinyl or wooden pets as props

Add unbreakable fish bowls for children to use in their constructions

Add signs to label pet stores and items to be found in pet stores

Dramatic Play

Add a real dog bed

Add a real pet dish

Add teacher-made or purchased pet masks

Add stuffed toy pets

Add empty pet food boxes, donated by parents, stuffed with crumpled paper and taped shut with clear tape

Science/Sensory Center

Examine a variety of pet foods

Make homemade dog biscuits

Care for live classroom pets

Add bird seed to the sensory table

Library Center

Add books about pets

Add pet puppets

Add flannel board stories about pets

Add read-along stories about pets to the listening area

Add pictures of pets along with their names to your word wall

Add pictures of pets along with their names printed on sentence strips in your ABC area

Manipulative Center

Provide pet puzzles

Add teacher-made folder games with pet themes

Music Center

Listen to tapes and CDs with songs about pets, including songs in children's home languages

Add teacher-made pet props, such as various types of tails attached to elastic bands to use for creative movement

Special activities could include visiting a pet shop, inviting a veterinarian to talk with the class about pet care, or inviting a parent to bring a pet for a visit. Transition activities could include moving like different types of pets, using pet-related finger plays, and singing and playing action songs about pets. Pictures around the room can feature various types of pets, including photos of children's own pets. Children will be literally immersed in the concept throughout the entire day and in every learning center.

Make the Classroom Familiar and Friendly

At the beginning of the school year, even the classroom is an unfamiliar place to children. Everything is new and stimulating. Because of this newness, it is important to keep the environment simple and basic. Spend the first few weeks of school simply helping the children understand how school works, where things are, and what to do when they are finished using something.

Children learn about new things by exploring them. What this means is that, for example, in the blocks center, blocks will be taken off the shelves, carried around, and dumped in piles on the floor. In the dramatic play center, all of the clothes, dishes, and other props will be taken out, examined, and piled together. The same type of exploratory behavior will take place throughout the classroom. So, keep each center simple, familiar, and easy for the children to manage. Provide only a few dress-up clothes, a couple of empty food containers, and a few dishes in the dramatic play center. Keep the blocks center simple, with just a few familiar props, such as figures of family members. Provide art activities that are easy and self-directing. Crayons, markers, paper, and simple stringing activities work best in the beginning of the year.

Look at your entire classroom and make sure that there is nothing that will require a great deal of adult supervision or assistance. Save the messy and elaborate project ideas for later in the year. The beginning of the school year is a time when you need to be free to help the children understand how to function in this new environment.

Develop Long-Range Plans

Look at a calendar of the whole school year and begin making some long-range plans. Keep in mind that you will want to begin with simple and familiar topics and gradually move toward new and complex projects. Many teachers choose to focus on simple, familiar ideas like "Introduction to School," "Me," "My Family," "My Home," "My Pets," or "My Friends" during the first four to six weeks of school.

Special Events

Next, look at the calendar for special events that occur in your school or in your community. For example, if your community hosts a festival every fall that is relevant to the lives and cultures of the children, you will want to include ideas about this event in your planning.

Seasons

Consider seasonal changes that will occur throughout the year when planning your curriculum. When the leaves start to turn and signs of fall appear, it may be time to explore characteristics of the fall season with your class. Work some of those activities into your long-range plans. Do the same with winter, spring, and summer.

Identify Skills to Develop

Make a list of knowledge and skills that you know you want to make sure the children develop, such as concepts related to safety, health, and nutrition. Also, get to know your students as individuals, assessing their knowledge, abilities, skills, and needs. Decide on the things that are important for your students to learn and keep them in mind as you plan lessons throughout the year.

Explore Children's Interests

Next, look at your students and families and use your K-W-L chart to help explore their interests. Most four-year-olds are fascinated with dinosaurs, for example. If this is the case with your class, be sure to include a project on dinosaurs in your plans. One of your students may have an interest in spiders. Your class could spend a fascinating week or more exploring that topic. Another student may have a special interest in trains. By tapping into that interest, your class could learn about various types of trains and maybe even take a short train trip to a neighboring community.

Special Topics

Finally, think about topics that are special to you. If you have a special area of expertise or a particular area of interest, share it with your students. A colleague of mine grew up on an island in the Caribbean, and she teaches a wonderful unit each year about her homeland. She shares foods, clothing, songs, and customs that are near and dear to her heart. Another colleague's family owns a heavy equipment business, so her class spends some time each year exploring the road-building machinery that is brought to the school parking lot. Be willing to share yourself with your students, and everyone will benefit.

Write Your Lesson Plans

The final step in curriculum planning is writing lesson plans. A lesson plan should include specific objectives as well as activities for group time, books for storytime, songs, and special activities. The plan should also include a list of activities for each learning center. You don't need to place all of the activities you have planned in each learning center all at once. Start with a few activities and add, take away, or rotate them as the project progresses, based on student needs and abilities. Some projects will last for a week or two, while others may last longer. Continue exploring the topic as long as it holds the children's interest and provides learning opportunities.

The lesson plan forms on pages 32–33 are designed to help you with this process. The first page is for your group activities. The second page is for your learning center activities. The names of the centers have been left blank intentionally so that you can personalize the form to fit your own unique classroom.

Document the Learning

Throughout the learning experience, take pictures, make posters, and encourage the children to dictate and draw about their accomplishments. Post some of these documents on the wall outside your classroom so that families can see what the children are learning. Post other documents inside the classroom—and at the children's eye level—so they can view and take pride in their work. Finally, bring your unit of study to a close and help the children identify and understand the learning that has taken place by finishing your K-W-L chart with them. The third column is "What We Learned." Write the children's ideas about what they learned about the topic during the course of the project. You might have a special celebration to which you invite parents or children and teachers from other classrooms to visit your room, look at your documentation, and talk with the children about their project. You may also want to put the photos, drawings, and dictation into a class-made book to keep in your library center for reflection.

Lesson Plan

Topic: _____ Objectives: _____

Dates: From _____ To _____ _____

	Monday	Tuesday	Wednesday	Thursday	Friday
Whole-Group Activities					
Books for Storytime					
Rhymes, Songs, Fingerplays					
Special Activities					
Materials					

Lesson Plan

Topic: _____   Dates: From _____ To _____

Learning Centers

Center	Activities
Materials	

Part II

Teaching Through the Environment With Learning Centers

Room Arrangement Basics

When you're planning your room arrangement, one way to approach the task is to consider the idea of dividing the room into regions. Within the regions there are zones, and within the zones, there are learning centers. As mentioned in the section "Planning the Curriculum," you will probably want to create at least seven basic centers and then add others as space and materials allow. The seven basic centers are art, blocks, dramatic play, science, library/literacy, manipulative, and music. The basic seven are used here but have been augmented with others that are listed separately but can be combined to equal the basic seven. Regardless of the size of your classroom or the number of centers you choose to create, there are certain guidelines to use when making decisions about the arrangement of your room.

Identify Regions

The first step is to identify your regions. There are two basic regions: wet and dry. Deciding which is which is really pretty simple. Ask yourself, "Where in this room will wet, drippy messes be most easily managed? Where is the flooring that is easily washable? Where is the sink? Where are the restrooms?" Wherever your answers point, there will be your wet region.

Next, ask yourself, "What area(s) of the room wouldn't be able to handle wet messes?" Where is the carpet? Where are the areas that are far away from the sink? This is your dry region. When you have located your regions, you're ready to identify zones and centers.

The Wet Region

Arrival Zone

If children and families enter your classroom directly from outdoors, then your arrival zone needs to be in a wet region where people can come in from all sorts of weather. When planning your arrival area, consider including the following components:

- A bulletin board for parent notices
- Cubbies or individual storage tubs
- A display of photos of children at play with their families (Framing the photos is a nice, homelike touch.)
- Displays of children's art work (As with the photos, framing or matting the children's work shows it off to its best advantage.)
- A bench and/or an adult-height counter to make it easier for parents to help children with their coats, rainboots, mittens, and other outdoor gear
- A counter for parents to sign children in and out
- A washable floor covering that can handle wet clothing and muddy shoes

Messy Zone

The other zone in your wet region is your messy area. The messy zone works best when it is located near a sink, with a washable floor covering that can take lots of drips and spills.

The centers to arrange in your messy zone include art, science, cooking, clay and dough, and sensory play.

Tables in these messy zone centers also serve nicely as dining tables for meals and snacks. Children's emerging self-help mealtime skills such as pouring their own milk and serving themselves family-style are much more easily managed in the messy zone!

The Dry Region

The dry region is usually best located in a carpeted area, away from the sinks and entrances. There are two zones in the dry region: active and quiet.

Active Zone

Active zone centers are those that tend to get rather noisy and require a fairly large amount of space. Active zone centers include blocks, construction, dramatic play, music, and woodworking. Children need plenty of room to construct, play, and move creatively in these areas.

Quiet Zone

Quiet zone centers are those that require less space because the activities there require less movement. In fact, if you are working

within a very small classroom, some of the quiet centers can be combined very successfully. Centers included in the quiet zone are the literacy centers (puppets, listening, library, writing, ABC, and computer), and the math and manipulatives center.

General Guidelines for Learning Centers

Organize Using Appropriate, Fun Materials

In every learning center, materials for the children's use need to be displayed in a neat and attractive manner on low, open shelves that are within children's reach. If you have pegs and pegboards, stringing beads, and colored cubes in the manipulative center, it's a good idea to place each type of equipment in its own container. Natural materials are nice, such as wicker baskets. If you prefer a more streamlined look in your classroom, clear plastic shoe boxes work well.

Be sure to label each container with both a picture and words, written in the proper combination of capital and lowercase letters. For example, consistently use a black marker for words in English and a blue marker for words in Spanish. Next, assign the container its own special place on a shelf with a matching label.

For some activities, you can also add a task card (see page 168), with photos or simple pictures and words explaining how to use the materials. The task cards not only help children understand how to use the items in the container, they also add a literacy component to every center in the room.

This type of organization takes time and effort, but the end result is well worth the effort. It enables children to find the materials they want, work with them independently, and return them in a neat and orderly manner. Children learn that there is a place and a purpose for everything. Early in the year, you'll need to check equipment at the end of each day to make sure that it has all been put away properly. After a few weeks, the children will be able to return materials with very little assistance.

Make Sure You Can Supervise All Centers

When creating your learning centers, consider whether you will be able to visually supervise activities in all the centers. Look around the room. Sit down in each center, as if you were working with a small group of children there. Can you see every other center in the room? If not, move shelves, furniture, and other obstacles out of the way. Use low shelves and dividers to keep your visual path clear at all times.

Plan for Traffic Flow

Consider traffic flow as you arrange your learning centers. Look at the way the centers are arranged in relation to one another. Children need to be able to move freely from center to center without interfering with other children's activities. If you have children who are in wheelchairs or who have challenges with mobility, consider those needs when placing your furniture and equipment. Think about the nature of the activities that will take place in each center. Some centers, like blocks, dramatic play, and library, tend to work best in corners.

Define Center Boundaries

Clearly define each center's space so that children and adults know where one center begins and another one ends. Clear boundaries also help confine specific types of activities to their own areas and prevent a confusing mixture of materials from adjoining centers. Area rugs make good center boundaries. Where the rug ends, the center ends. Colored tape lines on the floor can also define center boundaries. The arrangement of shelves and other pieces of furniture can create and define center boundaries. If you use a shelf to create a wall between centers, make sure the shelf has a back. Shelves that are open from both sides create confusion about which equipment belongs in which center. You also want to make sure that the shelf is sturdy and somewhat bottom heavy so that it won't tip over onto a child. If not, it is best to find a way to anchor it to the floor.

Using Signs

Center signs with words and pictures of center activities also help define learning centers. One way to do this is to suspend a mobile from the ceiling of each learning center. Be sure to hang it low enough for children to see it clearly. A triangle-shaped mobile, made from posterboard, is attractive, durable, and easy to make.

Try This

Making Mobiles

1. Cut out and fold a three-dimensional triangle.
2. Label and decorate it with items appropriate for the center. For example, an art center sign might have a paintbrush, a crayon, a glue bottle, and a pair of children's scissors, along with the words "Art Center."
3. Either glue the items onto the triangles (a hot glue gun works well) or suspend them on lengths of yarn, dangling below the triangles.

If you have children whose home languages are other than English, be sure to include their home languages in your classroom labeling, including on your center signs. Ask parents for help if you're not sure how to write the words you need. It helps children distinguish written languages if you consistently use different colors for each language.

Begin Designing!

Now that you have some general guidelines about learning center organization, you can begin designing your classroom. What centers will you create? Where will you locate each one? What specific activities will you provide in each learning center? What materials will you need for each activity? How will the activities change from day to day or from week to week? As you consider the answers to these and other questions, refer to the specific guidelines that follow for each learning center. You'll find practical, classroom-tested ideas for ways to set up, manage, and maintain your centers with ease. Each learning center description also ends with a list of helpful hints that highlight and recap the most important ideas to make your day (and the children's) flow smoothly.

4

Art Center

The art center is an ideal place for children to express themselves creatively and to explore various art materials. It will be appealing and inviting for many children and is especially important for those who have strong visual-spatial intelligence. This center is most effective when it is set up with a rich variety of open-ended art activities—activities with many possible outcomes.

Consider providing large sheets of plain paper, cups of bright, creamy tempera paint, and long-handled paint brushes. Some children might use all of the colors available and cover their paper with bright splashes of color. Other children may choose to paint a design. More mature children might paint a picture of something they have seen such as a house, a person, or a flower.

Giving children the freedom to make their own decisions and creatively communicate their ideas without a structured format will help them learn to express themselves and develop the skills they need as individuals.

Closed art activities that have a "right" and "wrong" way of being done are best saved for older grades. Examples of closed activities include coloring books, worksheets, and teacher-directed craft activities. In closed art activities, all the children's work ends up looking basically the same—a whole batch of adorable white bunnies with their cotton tails glued on in just the right place and their ears and noses colored pink. These types of activities can interfere with the young child's emerging ability to express thoughts, ideas, and feelings creatively!

Creating an Art Center

Essential Materials

Easel

An easel is an essential piece of equipment in the art center and should be accessible to painters every day. For the sake of mess management, place a shower curtain or shower curtain liner on the floor beneath the paint easel to catch drips and spills. Tape it securely to floor on all four sides so there won't be any loose edges that children could trip over. Using a color of tape that contrasts with the flooring helps create visual boundaries for the center.

Try This

Mess Management

Place a shower curtain or shower curtain liner on the floor beneath the paint easel to catch drips and spills.

You might also want to place a drying rack close to the easel—also on the shower curtain. When the drying area is close at hand, the children can easily take their wet paintings from the easel and place them on the rack or hang them up to dry. When there are many painters in one day, you might need to rearrange the paintings from time to time so that there is always space available for new masterpieces.

Tempera Paint

Tempera paint is one of the most popular types of paint for young children. It is nontoxic, inexpensive, and comes in many bright, bold, and beautiful colors. It is available in liquid and powder form. The powdered tempera paint is more economical, but will require some extra time on your part to mix. It is sometimes difficult to get the paint to be the consistency you want. Mixing three parts of powdered tempera paint to one part water usually achieves an acceptable consistency.

Placing paint in no-spill plastic paint cups, empty juice cans, individual milk cartons, or any other type of container that is deep enough to hold at least one day's supply of tempera paint will make your life easier than if the paints are in spillable cups. Be sure the containers are deep enough to hold a long-handled paintbrush without tipping over!

Paper

Keep a supply of paper available for children to use near the easel. Some easels come with rolls of paper attached. These are nice but not necessary. You can place large sheets of paper in an open box or plastic crate on the floor under or beside the easel. Children can then reach the paper easily and help themselves when they're ready to paint. It's also important to provide a variety of types and shapes of paper for the children. For specific suggestions, see Try This on this page.

Try This

Paper Options

Paper Types: Butcher paper, newspaper, wallpaper, leftover laminating film, and aluminum foil.

Paper Shapes: Circles, triangles, and squares. Try cutting out geometric shapes from the center of the paper to give the children experience working with negative space.

Pencils, Pens, and Markers

Keep a pencil, pen, or marker at the easel at all times. Attach it with a string or length of yarn to help keep it from "walking away." This enables the children to write their names or stories about their paintings without having to stop and find a writing tool. Even the very youngest child can make a mark of his or her own. A "signature" that may not be readable to you may have clear meaning to the child.

Tables

You also need a table or two in your art center. Covering a child-sized table with several layers of newspapers helps with mess management in the art center. When one layer of newspaper gets messy, roll it up and throw it away. A nice clean layer will appear underneath. Another approach is to cover the art table with a vinyl tablecloth with a thick flannel back. However, while a tablecloth protects the table from most clean-up problems, it does not provide an absorbent surface for wet spills.

Drying Space

You'll need to provide a drying space for finished art table projects. Some art activities will be non-messy, such as crayon drawings or bead stringing. These activities can go directly into a child's cubby or on the wall for display. Other projects may be drippy and messy for quite a while, and need a safe place where they can dry flat rather than hanging on the drying rack alongside the easel paintings. You can purchase drying racks at most school supply stores, or for the sake of economy, you can make your own drying racks.

Try This

Making Your Own Drying Racks

You'll need several large cardboard boxes that are all the same size. Cut the sides down so that you have shallow boxes. Stack them on top of each other and tape them together at the sides and back. Cut the fronts out so that you can slide the art papers into the box. Make the box more durable and attractive by covering it with self-adhesive plastic shelf paper.

Smocks

Young artists need access to paint smocks to protect their clothing (even though paint seems to have a way of finding its way under and around the best of smocks!). One easy way to remind children to wear smocks is to hang one at each painting space. To do this, screw vinyl-covered cup hooks into the sides of the easel for hanging smocks. You can also simply drape the smocks over the top of the easel. When the smocks visible and easy to reach, children are more likely to remember to put them on before they start painting.

Try This

Involving Parents

Ask parents to donate old shirts so you will have a good supply of paint smocks on hand.

Smocks can be purchased, you can make your own from vinyl fabric, or you can use men's cotton shirts worn with the buttons in the back. T-shirts don't work well as smocks, since they tend to absorb liquids and then pass those liquids through to the children's clothing underneath!

Paint smocks or shirts are a good idea for table art, too. One easy way to make them obvious and available to the children who are using the art table is to hang them over the backs of the chairs. This helps the children remember to wear the smocks before beginning a messy activity.

Shelves

Next, you'll need to have low, open shelves located near the art table. These shelves are for materials that children might need when they're working at the art table. Include a variety of open-ended art activities and the necessary supplies. One way to organize these items is to place each activity in a separate basket or tray. Using the

Keep in Mind calculation to determine the number of activities to offer, you might feel a bit overwhelmed! But keep in mind a couple of important reasons to provide a variety of art activities.

- Decision making

  When children have lots of options, they learn to make choices of their own and take responsibility for those choices. This is a giant step in developing thinking skills and a sense of self-confidence. Children are motivated to learn when they feel that they have some say about their own learning. Making choices about art activities helps them feel like they are in charge and is a great self-esteem booster.

- Skill building

  The variety of activities also helps you make sure that you are providing different types of skill-building experiences on various levels of development. You can have cutting activities, stringing activities, collages, drawing, painting, printing, and more available every day when you use a free-choice system.

Keep in Mind

Art Activities

A good rule of thumb to help ensure an appropriate number of activities is to multiply the number of children who can sit at the table at one time by 2½. If four children can sit at the art table, you would provide ten different activity choices. If six children can sit at the table, you need 15 activity choices.

Scissors Box

If your classroom is large enough, you might want to add a special scissors box to your art center. This is a great way to provide daily opportunities for cutting in an easy-to-manage style.

Invite children to go into the box and use the scissors to cut as much paper as they want. Scraps will fall on the floor of the box rather than all over your classroom. At clean-up time, encourage children to throw away scraps and tidy up the papers for future cutting experiences. This system is a friendly, neat, easy way to manage cutting practice. It's also fun for the children when they have their very own little house to enter for scissors work.

Try This

Scissors Box

Begin with a large cardboard box big enough for two children to sit in with plenty of work space to spare. Cut out a doorway and add baskets of paper and scissors for children to use.

Management Ideas

Preventing Messes

Most easels come equipped with a paint tray designed to hold paint cups. Some paint trays have holes for individual paint cups and others are trough-shaped. If your easel has a trough-shaped paint tray, stuff crumpled newspaper or newsprint around each paint cup to prevent messy spills. On some easels, there is a space between the paint trough and the paint board areas. If your easel is like this, stuff more crumpled paper into the space. These little precautions will save lots of clean-up time because the drips will go on the crumpled paper instead of on the floor.

Working With Paint

Tempera paint will sour if it is stored for a long time. You can avoid experiencing this unpleasant smell by mixing only enough paint to last about a week at a time. A Friday-afternoon-only clean-up job for the children can be to wash the paint cups with soapy water. Then they'll be fresh and ready for a new batch of paint on Monday morning.

Tempera paint can stain clothing. This is especially true of the brighter, stronger colors. To help prevent stains, try adding a small amount of liquid or powdered detergent to each cup of paint. This will also help stretch your tempera paint.

Guidelines for Center Users

To help children use the art center effectively, be sure to encourage them to:

❶ Wear a smock or paint shirt.

❷ Put the paintbrush back into the color where it started.

❸ Clean up spills when they happen.

❹ Work only on their own paper (unless the children have decided beforehand to collaborate on a project).

❺ Put things back where they found them when they are finished.

Using Paper

There are a number of ways to attach the paper to the easel for painting. You can use masking tape or clamps, but many teachers prefer spring-type clothespins. They are easier for the children to manage independently, especially if you clip three or four clothespins to the top of the easel for children to use.

Maintenance Checklist

The following is an actual, useable checklist for you to mark off each day. By reproducing the checklist and crossing off items when you've taken them into account, you'll keep your art center organized and fully stocked for another day of fun, educational experiences with art.

Teaching Tips

Listen Carefully

If children have a story to tell about their artwork, listen carefully. This can be done most effectively if you are on the same eye level as the children. Sit in a low chair or squat down so that the children know you are really "tuned in" to what they are saying. Encourage the children to "write" down their thoughts as well. It's OK if the "writing" is unreadable. What is important is the children's own awareness of the writing process.

Occasionally ask children if you can write, for them, the words they say. Write on a separate sheet of paper and not on the children's artwork. This is a way to show respect for the child's work and to provide a role model for writing "only on your own paper." When taking children's dictation, write the words exactly as they are spoken, without editing. When children see their own words being written down and hear them read back exactly as they were said, they begin to make the connection between oral language and written language. Children become aware that the mysterious thing called "reading" is just talk that's written down.

Encourage Children to Follow Through

Help children remember to see their work through to completion, especially in the first few weeks of school. This includes not only finishing their art but cleaning up spills and putting materials away. It might be quicker, neater, and easier for you to clean up after the children, but the outcome of encouraging children to be self-sufficient is far greater than achieving a tidy art center. Helping children learn to take responsibility for their own actions is a valuable lesson in life.

Daily Maintenance Checklist

☐ Check the paint supply and mix more paint if needed (or plan to have the paint helper do this job early in the day).

☐ Check the paper supply and put out more if needed.

☐ Remove dry paintings from the flat drying rack or line and file them or hang them on the wall at child's eye level.

☐ Make sure there are three or four clothespins at each painting space. Place the paintbrushes into the paint at the beginning of the day. Hang a paint smock at each painting space.

☐ Be sure that there is a pencil, pen, or marker at the easel.

☐ Cover the art table with a thick layer of newspaper or a vinyl tablecloth.

☐ Replenish materials in activity baskets as needed.

☐ Check glue bottles to be sure they are full and are flowing smoothly.

☐ At the end of the day, remove the paintbrushes from the paint, wash them, and store them with the bristles pointing up.

☐ Check the activity baskets for spills or messes. Remove messy newspaper layers from the art table.

Encourage Individuality and Creativity

In order to promote creative thinking, encourage children to invent their own ways of completing tasks or projects rather than telling or showing them how to do it. Try to avoid drawing for a child, telling a child how to draw something, or showing a child a model you've made. If you draw for children, they can feel discouraged because their efforts can never measure up to a product an adult has created.

If a child says, "I can't," "I don't know how," or "Draw it for me," you might respond by saying, "If I draw it, it will be my work and my ideas. This is your work and you need to do it your very own special way." You can talk with children about their ideas and help them find their own ways to express them. For example, if a child wants to draw a picture of a dog, ask the child to tell you about a dog. "How many legs does a dog have? How many ears?" You might also help the child find a photograph of a dog in a book or magazine in the classroom. Take the photograph to the art center for the child to use as a "live" model. By encouraging the children's self-expression, we support their emerging self-confidence and self-esteem, as well as helping them find their own unique ways to express creativity.

Choose Your Words Carefully

Choose your words carefully when talking to children about their art. Try to avoid asking children questions that put them on the spot. For example, a question that adults sometimes ask a child when looking at artwork is, "What is it?" A young child's art is often the result of experimenting with the materials and is not meant to be anything specific. On the other hand, if a child has worked very hard to represent a specific idea, he may feel discouraged by the fact that you cannot recognize it. When you talk with children about their art, you might simply say, "Tell me about your painting." This open-ended statement invites the child to respond in many ways. The child could say, "It's an elephant" or "I painted yellow." The pressure to give the "right" answer is eliminated.

Tips for Success: Remember to . . .

- ✰ Plan for and expect plenty of "mess" in the art center.

- ✰ Provide open-ended, creative art activities.

- ✰ Have all materials and equipment ready before the children arrive.

- ✰ Have extra materials on hand for replenishing as needed.

- ✰ Remind the children to return materials to their proper places when they are finished.

- ✰ Remind the children to return paintbrushes to their original paint cups in order to avoid mixing colors.

- ✰ Show children how to wipe paintbrushes on the sides of paint containers to avoid unwanted dripping.

- ✰ Show a genuine interest in the children's work.

- ✰ Encourage the children to practice self-help skills by putting on their own smocks, hanging up their own work to dry, and cleaning up after themselves.

- ✰ Encourage children to write about their creations or offer to take dictation when they tell about their work.

- ✰ Write on a separate piece of paper or on an index card, not on the child's artwork.

- ✰ Allow children to decide how much time they will spend in the art center and how many works of art they will create each day.

5

Blocks Center

The blocks center is a very important part of an early childhood classroom. In fact, if you had to choose one center in the classroom as the most important of all, the blocks center would be a prime candidate for the title. When children build with blocks, they learn about mathematical concepts such as size, shape, number, and quantity. They become aware of scientific principles such as the force of gravity and the functioning of simple machines such as levers and inclined planes. They learn to think, plan, and problem-solve as their structures take form. This center has special appeal for children whose intelligences are strong in the visual/spatial, logical/mathematical, and bodily/ kinesthetic areas.

Blocks play provides children with opportunities to create, cooperate, and communicate. *Social learning* takes place in the blocks center as children work together to share materials, space, and ideas. *Literacy skills* develop through block play when children write signs for their buildings and read teacher-made task cards for various blocks experiences. Children gain *eye-hand coordination* and *visual discrimination* skills when they group blocks that are the same size and shape at clean-up time. Virtually everything you might want to teach a young child can be taught through blocks play!

Creating a Blocks Center

Space and Location

The most important consideration in planning a blocks center is space. Since children need plenty of space to build creatively, a blocks center will take up a sizable area in your classroom. Ideally, the blocks center should be in a corner of the room that gets little traffic. This out-of-the-way placement will help prevent many of the disasters that occur when passers-by accidentally bump into structures that have been created with care.

Essential Materials

Rug

Placing a rug with low nap on the floor of the blocks center serves several purposes. It defines the space and outlines the boundaries for blocks play. It provides a comfortable surface for the children to work on since they will be sitting, kneeling, and crawling about on the floor while they construct. The rug is also a good sound absorber. It helps muffle the sound of falling blocks when structures topple over.

Shelves, Not Bins

The blocks center needs low, open shelves for storing blocks when they are not in use. The shelves need to be open and accessible to the children during learning center activity time. Blocks storage bins are available in some early childhood equipment catalogs and stores. While these bins are convenient to have if you need to store blocks over an extended vacation or when things are being moved around for cleaning and maintenance work, they are not generally recommended for regular classroom use.

One problem with keeping blocks in a bin or box is that children have to "dig" through all the blocks to find the shapes and sizes they need for their buildings. This is frustrating to children, and it creates an incredible amount of noise and unnecessary clutter with all the discarded blocks scattered around the floor. Blocks building is encouraged when children can see, at a glance, which shapes and sizes are available for their buildings. Another problem with storage bins is that they fail to give the children the message that the blocks center is a place with a purpose and a sense of order. Whenever materials are dumped together in a random way, the unspoken (and unintended) message is, "This stuff isn't very important and it doesn't need to be handled with care." Help children understand that everything in the classroom is valuable and important enough to be treated with respect.

Unit Blocks

The main feature of the blocks center is a set of high-quality wooden unit blocks (preferably several hundred that include a variety of different shapes and sizes). Unit blocks are available commercially in classroom sets. These blocks are mathematically related to each other. For example, the basic unit is a rectangle. Two square blocks equal one unit. Two narrow rectangles equal one unit. Two right triangles equal one unit, and so on. While many classroom materials can be homemade, it is usually best to purchase commercially made wooden unit blocks. The perfect fit that is required tends to be very difficult for the home woodworker to achieve. While a classroom set of unit blocks is a large expense, the blocks are virtually indestructible and can be expected to last for many, many years.

Additional Props

Once these basic components of the blocks center are in place, consider adding additional props. For example, add wooden people figures, cars, trucks, and traffic signs. You can change the props to fit project themes or units of study. Just like the blocks, the props need a special place to "live" when block play is over for the day. To reserve a space on the shelves, mark the desired area with a simple sign that says "props."

Try This

Create Boundaries for Building

Use colored tape or masking tape to create a line on the rug about two feet away from the shelf and as long as the shelf. When you encourage children to build structures on the side of the tape line away from the shelf, this makes the space between the line and the shelf available for traffic. Children can get to the shelves to get more blocks without interfering with anyone else's buildings—and lots of conflicts are avoided!

Try This

Signs for Props

Within the prop area of the blocks center, make a sign with pictures and words for each type of prop. Not only do the signs help keep the area organized, they make the blocks center an important part of a print-rich environment.

To enhance their development of mathematical concepts through blocks play, provide such measuring tools as tape measures, rulers, lengths of yarn or ribbon, rolls of adding machine paper, and cutouts of hands and feet at the blocks center. It is usually wise to start out with only one or two of the measuring tools and change or add others as the year progresses. Just as with your other props, identifying a specific spot on a low shelf to store the measuring tools will help with the smooth operation of the center.

Writing Materials

Writing materials such as index cards and pencils are also a necessary part of the blocks center. When you designate a spot on a shelf to store the writing materials and label it clearly, you have tools to encourage children's emerging writing skills. They can make signs and write stories about their buildings. Make sure you have tape available so the children can attach their written work to their constructions.

Keep in Mind

Make It Viewable

Be sure to place the visual aids at the children's eye level so that they will be most useful and accessible to children as they work.

Visual Aids

Inspiration for creative buildings can come from displaying a few carefully selected photographs or realistic posters that depict children working with blocks or various types of buildings and structures.

Task Cards

The final step to creating your blocks center is to add task cards. These are simple drawings or photographs, accompanied with words, of the actual children in your classroom. Task cards show children how to use materials. A basic set of task cards should always be on display in the blocks center. For example, a set of task cards might show a 3-step sequence for blocks play: (1) choose the blocks, (2) build with the blocks, (3) put the blocks away. Include task cards that show children how to use the measuring tools and writing materials. Other task cards can be added throughout the year to go along with

Try This

Using Task Cards

When teaching about farm life, place a set of task cards in the blocks center that shows children how they might build an animal pen.

particular themes or projects. For additional information, see the section on "Task Cards" on page 168.

Management Ideas

Make Block Outlines

Each different type of block should have its own special place on a shelf. One way to make the blocks center an attractive place for play, along with giving the children an opportunity to match and sort by shape and size, is to use blocks outlines. Using construction paper or posterboard, trace around each different block shape and size to make a pattern and cut the patterns out. Another approach is to put the blocks on a copier or scanner and make a copy of each shape and size. Be sure to laminate the outlines or copies for the sake of durability. Next, tape or glue the laminated outlines to the shelves or on the back of the bookcase just above the shelves to show where each type of block goes at clean-up time.

Guidelines for Center Users

When children visit the blocks center, encourage them to:

❶ Build only as high as their shoulders. (This protects children's heads from injury when block buildings fall, and they will!)

❷ Build on the side of the tape line that is away from the shelf.

❸ Take down only their own buildings.

❹ Put their blocks away before they leave the center. (This rule may not be necessary in your classroom. In some situations, blocks buildings can remain standing overnight or for several days.)

❺ Take blocks buildings down with their hands, not their feet.

❻ Match the blocks to the shapes on the shelves and put them away.

Begin Clean-Up Early

It is usually wise to begin clean-up work a few minutes earlier in the blocks center because putting away hundreds of blocks can be quite time consuming. If you get involved and help children put blocks on the shelves, it is a less daunting task for them, especially during the first weeks of school. Asking children to show you where to put the blocks helps them gain experience matching blocks with the outlined shapes and provides you with the opportunity to teach the names of various shapes.

Daily Maintenance Checklist

☐ Check the shelves to make sure all the blocks are in place.

☐ Periodically check the silhouettes, signs, and task cards to make sure they are firmly attached and are in good condition. Reattach or replace them as needed.

☐ Check cars, trucks, and other accessories for missing wheels and broken parts.

☐ Remove any broken equipment from the center until it can be repaired.

☐ Check the writing materials and replenish the supplies as needed.

Teaching Tips

Respect Developmental Stages

Keep in Mind

Observe Quietly

Try to resist the urge to hurry children along by teaching them how to build better structures. When children are in the exploratory stage, stay in the background and observe their explorations.

Children pass through several predictable stages during blocks play. Being aware of these stages will help you discover ways to support their play. In the initial stages, children need to *explore* the nature of blocks. They need to experience the texture, weight, and shape of blocks. To do this, children will often cart blocks around the center, moving them from one messy pile to another. This may not look much like blocks building, but it is a necessary stage. After awhile, they will begin to actually build structures.

Children may first lay the blocks end to end flat on the rug. Later, they might begin to build upward, stacking blocks on top of each other. Eventually, children will build enclosures, bridges, and elaborate structures that have many interesting features. Be patient and remember that children go through each stage in their own time and in their own way.

Talk With Children About Their Ideas

While children are busy at play, talk with them about their ideas. The following comments speak specifically about structural features, and they are a great way to teach concepts related to shape, size, and number in an easy, informal way:

- "I see that you used a lot of triangles in your building."
- "Your building is high in some places and low in some places."
- "You used some long rectangles and some short rectangles."
- "There's a big square that you made with four rectangles."

Ask Open-Ended Questions

Ask open-ended questions such as, "How did you make this building?" or "How many blocks do you think you'll need for your building?" to stretch students' thinking skills. See Bloom's Taxonomy on page 23 for more ideas for questioning.

Encourage Literacy

Be sure the children know where the writing materials are and encourage them to make their own signs to go with their blocks creations. If children don't seem interested in writing the signs themselves, you might inspire them by asking them to dictate their ideas to you. If you are doing the writing, be sure to print neatly and write the child's own words exactly as they are spoken. One good way to stimulate sign-making is as a response to a child who says, "I want to leave my building up. Don't let anyone knock it down." Instead of promising to protect a building, suggest that the child make a sign to put on the building to communicate the thought. This idea is generally appealing to young children, and you will probably find many "Do not knock down" signs being attached to their buildings.

Provide Appropriate Materials

Be alert and responsive to children's needs as they build with the blocks. If, for example, you see that children need a roof for a structure and there are no blocks big enough to do the job, bring out some sheets of cardboard or swatches of fabric and take them to the blocks center. Or you might invite the builders to go with you on an "exploring" visit to the storage closet where they can work with you to find the materials they need.

Ensure Safety and Guide Behavior

Keep a watchful eye for safety hazards and guide behavior in the blocks center. The task cards are a great help in doing this job. Instead of telling children what not to do, invite them to read the directions for blocks building. For example, if a child is scraping all the blocks off the shelf and tossing them around the center, take the child to the task cards and help "read" the directions for using blocks. Point out the number of blocks that the task card shows being taken off the shelf at one time. Then go on to the next step in the task cards, which is using the blocks for building.

 # Tips for Success: Remember to . . .

- ✿ Make sure all equipment and materials are in order before school.
- ✿ Show a genuine interest in the children's blocks work.
- ✿ Ask open-ended questions to stimulate thinking and creativity.
- ✿ Comment on specific things you notice about children's structures.
- ✿ Encourage children to make signs for their buildings.
- ✿ Be available to write signs for children.
- ✿ Print children's words in manuscript print, exactly as they are spoken.
- ✿ Help children put blocks away in their designated places on low, open, labeled shelves during clean-up time.
- ✿ Allow extra time for blocks center clean-up.
- ✿ Help children get materials they need to add to blocks buildings.
- ✿ Accept the children's developmental stages of blocks building.
- ✿ Use task cards to help guide behavior.

Dramatic Play Center

Some teachers call the dramatic play center the "home center" or "housekeeping center." Don't let the word "play" mislead you! The dramatic play center is a place where genuine learning takes place. Far from being a place to go to play when the "real work" is done, dramatic play is a vital part of a well-rounded curriculum in the classroom for young children. It may be of special interest to children who are especially strong in inter-personal and/or linguistic intelligences. Social studies concepts are learned through dramatic play. Children learn about various adult roles in the family and the community. Social skills develop as children learn to negotiate roles, share materials, and work cooperatively in order to make the play progress. Mathematical concepts are also learned through dramatic play. For example, when a child matches a cup to a saucer or a napkin to a plate, the concept of one-to-one correspondence is being learned. Counting the

59

number of plates needed to set the table for the "family" is a practical way to develop counting skills. Oral language develops when children share ideas and communicate with each other during their play.

Children's vocabularies increase when they play with new materials and learn the meanings of new words. Literacy emerges when they write grocery lists, telephone messages, and notes to put on the bulletin board in the play kitchen. Cookbooks, telephone books, task cards, and other reading materials give children an opportunity to interact with print through their play. And, fine motor development is encouraged when children use their fingers to fasten buttons and snaps on dress-up clothes.

Try This

Mops and Brooms

Cut the handles on real mops and brooms to a shorter length to make them child-size and manageable.

Keep in Mind

Cultural Diversity

Make sure that your cooking equipment, dishes, and foods reflect the children's cultures. One great way to do this is to ask families to send in their empty food boxes from home.

Try This

An Inexpensive "Bed"

An old dresser drawer filled with a small blanket and a pillow makes for a great bed.

Creating a Dramatic Play Center

If space is available, it is helpful to divide a dramatic play center into two areas: the kitchen and the bedroom.

The Kitchen

The kitchen area may be furnished with a child-size play sink, stove, refrigerator, hutch or cabinet for dishes, and table and chairs. Other additions might include a doll-size high chair, a child-size ironing board and iron, mops, and brooms. Lightweight pots and pans, unbreakable dishes, forks, spoons, table knives, plastic foods, empty food boxes and cans, and paper and pencils round out the materials that are needed for a great dramatic play kitchen area.

The Bedroom

In the bedroom area, provide a bed that is large enough and sturdy enough to hold a child. Children tend to get into the beds during their dramatic play, and a bed that is too small or a flimsy doll bed will quickly get broken. Other items to furnish the bedroom include a sturdy child-size rocking chair, a dressing table, an unbreakable full-length mirror, a chest of drawers, and low, open shelves for dress-up clothes. A wardrobe or an area for hanging clothes is also nice to have. If you have access to an aluminum chart stand, turn it on its side, add coat hangers, and you have a great place to hang dress-ups. Easy-to-manage dress-up clothes for male and female roles include purses, wallets, shoes, hats, and wigs. Empty plastic cologne and after shave lotion bottles, costume jewelry, hand mirrors, bedding, baby dolls with various skin tones, doll clothes, baby toys, real telephones, paper and pencil, and an assortment of books for bedtime stories round out the equipment list for the bedroom.

Keep in Mind

Cultural Diversity

Asking parents to donate old clothes for dress-up play is a way to ensure that children see their families and their cultures reflected in the classroom.

Transforming the Center

The basic "home living" setup is the most common way to arrange your dramatic play center. However, as time goes by, keeping the same setup all of the time may become less interesting to the children. You'll keep interest high if you periodically remove or change the furniture to create a new play environment.

If your class is studying firefighters, you and the children can transform the dramatic play center into a fire station. Remove some of the furniture or turn it to the wall and cover it with butcher paper. Add a cardboard box that you and the children have transformed into a "fire engine," large enough for the children to get into and "drive." Add dress-up clothes such as helmets, rubber boots, and raincoats. A task card that explains how to be a firefighter, labels for the new equipment on the shelves, and a sign to identify the fire station will invite the children to try new and challenging play experiences.

Keep in Mind

There's No Place Like Home

Always return to the home living setup for awhile before you make another change. The children need the security of that familiar environment and the opportunities it provides to play out important family themes.

Change the play environment throughout the year to go along with various projects. You and the children can have great fun turning your dramatic play center into a bakery, a grocery store, an auto mechanic shop, a farm, a beach, or a space station.

Define Places and Spaces

When you set up the center, make sure that there is a clearly defined place for everything. The dramatic play center, just like all the other areas in the classroom, needs to have an air of order and purpose. One simple and neat way to store dress-up accessories is in plastic laundry baskets that fit on a shelf.

Labeling

Use index cards to make labels that have pictures of the types of materials that go in the baskets and the words to describe the materials. For example, draw a picture of various types of hats on an index card or take a picture of the hats that go into the basket and tape it onto the card. Neatly print the word "hats" on the card. Attach the label to the front of the basket and place the basket on the shelf. This type of organization helps children know where to find the hats and where to put them when their play is finished. For prekindergartners and kindergartners, these cards provide a "reading" opportunity. Similar baskets can be used to store shoes and boots, purses and wallets, hair items (wigs, combs, curling irons with the cords removed, rollers), and baby items (rattles, bottles, diapers).

The same type of labeling is useful in the kitchen area to identify the places for pots and pans, dishes, cleaning tools, fruits and vegetables, refrigerator items, and canned and boxed foods. Attach these labels to the furniture itself. For example, attach the sign that says "refrigerator things" directly to the refrigerator door and the "dishes" sign directly on the hutch.

Task Cards

Task cards can help children get started with purposeful play. For example, a basic task card for child care might show a child picking up a doll, sitting in a rocking chair, and giving the doll a bottle. Other beginning task cards can show the children how to wash dishes and put them away or how to use dress-up clothes. You can make your own task cards with simple stick figures or photos of the actual children in the classroom using the materials on hand. For more information on making task cards see "Task Cards" on page 168.

Management Ideas

Affordable resources for obtaining props include yard sales, flea markets, and especially, parents! By sending a "beautiful junk" list to parents at the beginning of the school year and asking them to send various household discards to school such as old clothes, dishes, pots and pans, and appliances, you'll collect a "treasure trove" of dramatic play materials. Just make sure that all donated or "found" items are safe, nontoxic, and have no sharp edges or broken parts that could present a safety hazards.

Guidelines for Center Users

When children visit the dramatic play center, encourage them to:

❶ Put things away in their proper place when they finish using them.

❷ Keep dramatic play materials and equipment in the dramatic play center. (Be flexible with this guideline. For example, children might visit between the block and the dramatic play centers. In this case, dress-up clothes can be worn in both places.)

Daily Maintenance Checklist

☐ Check the baskets, shelves, hooks, and drawers to see that everything is in its place.

☐ Check to see if everything is in good condition. If you find anything that is torn or broken, repair it or remove it from the center until it can be repaired.

☐ Take the dress-up clothes home for laundering from time to time.

Teaching Tips

Change Props and Themes

Changing the dramatic play center at the beginning of the year is primarily an adult job and can be done before or after school, when the children are not in the room. Express your own creativity and provide wonderful discovery experiences for the children.

Involving Children

As time goes by and the children gain maturity and experience with new environments, you may want to involve them in making the changes. Their involvement should be gradual. First, have them put props and materials in storage boxes when it's time to transform the center into something new. Once you and the children are comfortable with this, it's fine to move on to the next step: setup. Involve the children in setting up the center by inviting them to choose places on the shelves for new props, attaching the new labels to the baskets, and posting the new task cards. This involvement requires a lot of planning on your part. Have all the labels, task cards, equipment, and materials ready to go before you invite the children to participate in setting up the dramatic play center.

The final step involves having the children plan the environment themselves. This is accomplished most effectively after children have had lots of experiences with the other stages of involvement. It is usually best done near the end of the school year. At this stage, the children start with a piece of paper and an idea and brainstorm a list of things they will need.

For example, if your class visits a florist shop, children may be inspired to set up a florist shop in the dramatic play center. Sit in the dramatic play center with a small group of children and ask them what they would need to do to change the center into a florist shop. Have a pencil and paper handy and make a list of their ideas as well as the materials and equipment they need. In this case, children might suggest they will need a work table, a desk with a cash register and paper for taking orders, a telephone, some storage shelves, vases, ribbons, flowers, aprons for workers to wear, scissors, tape and cards for the customers to use to write messages with their flower orders, a sign for the store, and a price list for the flowers. You might then suggest that children use boxes labeled with color words to sort flowers by color.

As children progress, your role may shift from advisor to assistant. Help children find the materials they need and review their original list from time to time to make sure everything is accomplished. The process may take several days. Be sure to tap community resources when searching for materials. For example, a parent who makes silk flower arrangements as a hobby may be willing to donate extra boxes of flowers, ribbon, or floral tape. Encourage children to use the materials they have gathered and arrange them to accomplish their goals. Children can sort the flowers, make signs and labels, and cut up index cards into smaller cards for the customers to send with their flowers. They can dictate what they would like printed and drawn on task cards. Finally, when the store opens for business, the children will have a wonderful, productive play environment. This level of child involvement is a terrific end product of several years of exposure to well-prepared dramatic play environments.

Assist During Clean-Up

In the early weeks of the school year, expect that children will need help finding the right places for everything. Allow plenty of time for cleaning up. Ask the children to help find the places for things at clean-up time instead of quickly and efficiently putting things away yourself. Spend some time helping children think through the logic of the center's arrangement. For example, if a child begins to put the dolls in the refrigerator, ask where people sleep at his or her home and help the child arrive at the conclusion that the bed is a more appropriate place for dolls.

If there's a lot of cleaning up to do, make it more palatable by breaking it down into small tasks. Use the shelf and basket labels as tools to help clean-up work go smoothly. For example, get the shoe and boot basket, look at the picture label with a child, and ask that child to find all the things that go in that particular basket. Suggest that another child be in charge of collecting all of the pots and pans. As time goes by, the children will be able to take over more of the responsibility, and your help will be needed less often.

Respect Developmental Stages

Dramatic play is an interesting activity for adults to observe. Young children pass through predictable stages in their dramatic play, just as they do in their blocks play.

The Manipulative Stage

The manipulative stage comes first. This is a time for exploring the materials and equipment. Adults who aren't prepared for this may find themselves quite frustrated. During the manipulative stage, children take all of the wonderful materials you have put into the center and dump them together into a heap on the floor, pile them all onto the bed, stuff them into a suitcase, or carry them around the center with no apparent purpose or meaning. There's usually not much creative pretending happening during this stage, although the children might say things like, "We're moving," or "We're going on a picnic," while they're dumping everything together. What's really going on is that the children are finding out what's available and how it all works.

To make your life easier, start the school year expecting that at least some of the children will be in the manipulative stage. This is especially true for the prekindergarten classroom. Plan for this by putting out only a few basic materials for the first few weeks of school. Make sure that everything that is provided is simple and sturdy. For example, instead of beginning with a complete set of dishes and silverware, put out only four plates, four cups, and four spoons. Instead of providing a rich variety of dress-up clothes, start with four very simple pieces of clothing that are easy to take on and off. Since you will expect piling and dumping, if you provide a suitcase with easy fasteners, the children will have a place to put everything.

The Functional Stage

As time goes by and the children's experience base grows, dramatic play becomes more creative and purposeful. The children move into the functional stage—the stage at which they start using the materials in a realistic, functional way. They use the mop to mop the floor, put the dishes on the table, and feed the doll in the high chair. They also begin taking on familiar family roles in their play and act out those roles as they see appropriate.

Recognize Children With Limited Experiences

At the beginning of the school year, some children may appear to have limited imaginations. Children who come to school with very limited experiences in the world have had little to feed their imaginations. Without interesting, enriching life experiences, there's not much of a base for imaginative play. During the year, focus on providing interesting experiences on which children can build their play. But, to get children started right from the beginning, introduce children to the familiar—the home living equipment. While some children may have no idea what a firefighter or a zookeeper does, they have some concept of what families do in a kitchen and a bedroom. Use as many realistic props as possible. For example, provide a real iron (with the cord removed) rather than a wooden play iron. Use real pots, pans, and dishes so children can play at cooking. And provide an unbreakable, real baby bottle and realistic looking dolls to encourage children to dramatize child care.

Listen and Observe

You can learn a lot about children, their view of themselves, and their relationships with family members through careful listening and observation. For example, Joey was a four-year-old boy who played and behaved very aggressively toward other children. His play was especially rough with the girls in the class. By observing Joey in the dramatic play center, his teacher gained insight into his behavior. When Joey played the role of daddy, he sat in a chair, leaned back, barked orders, and growled criticisms. It appeared that the model Joey had at home was one of a dominant male figure. By understanding the basis for Joey's behavior, the teacher was able to find ways to help Joey grow in his awareness of positive, mutually respectful relationships among family members.

Intervene When Needed

If the children seem to be having a hard time initiating pretend play, join in to stimulate ideas. Pretend to be a neighbor or a grandparent who has dropped by for a visit. Sit down at the table and mention that you are really hungry. Start conversations by asking what will be served for dinner, how the baby is feeling, or if you can help wash the dishes. Pretend with the children for just a little while until the children are ready to pick up the pretend play on their own.

This type of intervention can also be helpful if there is one child who wants to join in a group's play but doesn't know how to go about it. Offer to be the child's mother or father for a while and take the child with you to visit the neighbors. Introduce the child to the group at play. Help the child enter the play by suggesting things he or she might do. For example, you might say, "Drew is such a good babysitter. Could he help you take care of your baby today?" When the reluctant child has been accepted into the play group, you can step away.

Don't Overstay Your Welcome

It's important to note that the purpose of joining in children's play is just to get them started. As soon as they are able to continue the play on their own, remove yourself from the scene. The goal is to help children learn how to work and play independently, not to be their playmate! Children need the security of knowing that you can be counted on to behave in a mature, responsible fashion. It can be frightening and confusing to young children to see adults acting like children. Also, it becomes impossible for children to use their own ideas and direct their own play if an adult is involved for too long a period of time.

Anticipate Needs

Be available as a resource and provider for the children's dramatic play. Carefully observe what children might need as they play. If you notice that children are putting the dolls in the kitchen sink with the dishes, bring out a baby bathtub, towels, and washcloths so that the baby can be given a proper bath. If children seem frustrated by the limited number of dishes and dress-up clothes, bring out more variety to enrich their play.

Tips for Success: Remember to . . .

 ✯ Provide a place for everything.
 ✯ Provide picture and written labels for all equipment.
 ✯ Provide task cards to help children get started with their play.
 ✯ Provide real appliances, dishes, and so on.
 ✯ Observe children carefully during their play and make notes about significant observations.
 ✯ Enter into the children's play when you see that help is needed. Remove yourself from the play when you see that help is no longer necessary.

★ Help the children use pictures and written labels to find the right places for materials at clean-up time.

★ Provide equipment and materials as the children show a need for them.

★ Expect some "manipulative stage" play when school first starts.

★ Limit the number and variety of materials available when school first starts.

★ Add materials when children are ready for more variety.

★ Change the theme of the center from the basic home living theme when you see that the children are ready for a change. Look for ways to include the children in planning and creating a new environment.

★ Remember to always return to the home living setup for awhile before you make another change.

Literacy Centers

A variety of centers in your classroom can provide students with rich opportunities to develop oral language and literacy skills. This chapter looks in depth at six centers:

Puppet Center

Listening Center

Library Center

Writing Center

ABC Center

Computer Center

Puppet Center

Puppets are a wonderful way for children to develop oral language skills and to learn to express their ideas and feelings. Puppets are especially helpful for children who feel unsure of themselves. Talking through a puppet can help children say things that are hard to say face to face. Children can act out favorite stories, make up puppet plays of their own, and work through all kinds of problems and challenges through puppet play.

Creating a Puppet Center

A puppet center can be very large and fancy or it can be small and simple, depending upon the space and equipment you have available.

Essential Materials

Puppet Theater

Some classrooms have plenty of space and can be set up with a permanent puppet theater. But even if space is limited, it's important to have a puppet theater, if only for performance days. Puppet theaters can be purchased from school supply stores or you can make your own. One easy way to make a puppet stage is to stretch a spring-type curtain rod across a doorway or in a corner of the room. Hang a dark curtain from the rod. Make sure it is low enough so that the children can sit on the floor or in child-sized chairs and reach the "stage" with their puppets.

Puppets

Provide a variety of puppets throughout the year to keep the center interesting and attractive to the children. Simple puppets, such as sock puppets, finger puppets, paper bag puppets, and stick puppets can be made by adults and children. More elaborate puppets can be purchased at school supply stores, at many education conferences, or in stores that specialize in puppets. While puppets tend to be fairly expensive, a quality puppet will last for many, many years. If you can, buy puppets with mouths that can be manipulated. These puppets can then show many different emotions. They can smile, frown, laugh, cry, sneeze, burp, yawn, and show fear, surprise, anger, and more. If you cut a small hole in the puppet's mouth, it can even eat!

Keep in Mind

Puppet Shopping

The most useful puppets are those with flexible mouths.

Management Ideas

If space is limited in your classroom, incorporate puppets into another center such as the listening center (page 75) or library center (page 80). All you need for a simple puppet area is a large laundry basket to hold the puppets. Label the basket using a picture of puppets and the word "Puppets." This will help the children know where to put the puppets at clean-up time. Simply turning the basket on its side creates a makeshift puppet stage.

Guidelines for Center Users

When children choose to visit the puppet center, encourage them to:

❶ Keep puppets in the puppet center.

❷ Return the puppets to the basket when they are finished playing.

Daily Maintenance Checklist

☐ Check to make sure the puppets are in good condition. Be sure that puppets have been put away properly.

☐ Check homemade puppets periodically and replace them when they begin to show wear.

☐ Mend small holes or tears immediately to prevent further damage.

☐ Remove torn or damaged puppets from the center.

Teaching Tips

Expect Free Exploration

Some children may have had experience using puppets, but others will find puppets a new idea. It might take some time and practice before these children are comfortable using puppets appropriately. As with most new ideas, children will go through an exploratory stage. They will put sock puppets or paper bag puppets on, take them off, and examine the different kinds of puppets inside and out until they understand the physical aspects of the puppets. If you anticipate this kind of free exploration, you will help the children reach a point at which they can begin using the puppets to acting out stories and express ideas and emotions.

Investigate Inappropriate Puppet Play

Some young children begin puppet play by using the puppets in an aggressive way. The puppets fight with each other, and the flexible mouths are used for biting. If you notice this type of play in your puppet center, place a puppet on your hand and join in the play. Use your puppet to talk to the other puppets. Ask them why they are angry or why they want to hurt each other. You might discover that there are some very strong emotions that need to be talked about. If the biting and fighting continues, use your puppet to tell the others that you don't like to be hit or bitten. Encourage children to find more positive ways to play. Use your puppet to suggest acting out a story or begin a friendly type of interaction like talking about favorite foods or places to visit.

Keep in Mind

Puppet Play

Puppets are often used by children as a psychologically safe way to express difficult emotions.

Coordinate Puppets With Project Themes

Use your project themes as a guide for choosing puppets to add to the puppet center. When you are studying insects, for instance, you might add bee, butterfly, and ladybug puppets to the center. When you study pets, you can provide dog and cat puppets. Some basic puppets, such as family member puppets, should always be on hand. Family member puppets enable children to work on personal and family issues throughout the year.

Encourage Puppet Productions

Coordinating the puppet center with literacy center themes encourages productive play with the puppets. If, for example, you have the story of *Goldilocks and the Three Bears* on the book shelf, you might provide three bear puppets and a Goldilocks puppet in the puppet center. Offer to be the narrator for the story and help the children get started by inviting them to choose their roles and act out the story. Be prepared for children to take creative license. The story might change significantly from that in the book. Remain flexible and ready to follow the children's lead in their productions. If interest is high, you might invite the children to perform their play for audiences such as other classmates, children from other classrooms, school administrators, or anyone else you can find on the spur of the moment. This type of on-the-spot performance can be fun and enriching for everyone involved. The children can write invitations, set up chairs or other seating arrangements, and pop popcorn or prepare some other type of refreshment for the "guests." Be careful not to get directive and take away the magic by turning it into an adult-centered program.

Tips for Success: Remember to . . .

 ✭ Talk with the children's puppets in a casual, informal way.

 ✭ Join in the play with your own puppet when you see that the play is aggressive or that the children need some ideas for puppet conversation.

 ✭ Provide a variety of puppets to complement your theme or unit of study.

 ✭ Keep puppets clean and in good repair.

 ✭ Offer to facilitate a puppet play by serving as the narrator for a story.

 ✭ Occasionally invite the children to show a puppet play to others and help make the necessary arrangements.

Listening Center

Today's society is filled with noise. Many homes have television on from morning through night as constant background noise. Music, loud speakers, and other mechanical sounds can be heard everywhere we go. With all of the noise pollution in our world, many young children learn at an early age to "tune out" many of the sounds that surround them. Because of this, one of the most important tasks in the early childhood classroom is teaching children to listen. The ability to listen carefully is an important prerequisite to later success in school. It is especially important for children to be able to develop phonological awareness (the ability to distinguish the sounds of language) in order to be ready to learn to read. The listening center is a place where children can go to acquire this essential skill.

Creating a Listening Center

The listening center may be its own center in a quiet area of the classroom or it may be a part of one of the literacy centers, such as the library center (see page 80).

Essential Materials

Just a few pieces of equipment are necessary for a successful listening center. Provide a table and chairs, tape recorder or CD player, headphones, storybook tape or CD sets, and a container to hold the books and tapes or CDs. Excellent, inexpensive paperback books and tapes or CDs are available from many early childhood book clubs. *Be sure to order at least two copies of each book.* If you have more than two headsets, order more books so that each child who is listening to a story can have a personal copy of the book.

Try This

> ### Color Coding Equipment
>
> Color code the buttons on CD or tape players using colored tape or stickers. Mark the "play" button with green, the "stop" button with red, and, for a tape player, code the "rewind" button with yellow.

As with all areas of the classroom, the listening center is most effective if it is child-directed. Expect the children to need some help in the first few weeks of school, but they will quickly learn to manage the tape recorder/CD player independently if you prepare the environment carefully. Make a task card with stick figures or actual photos of the player in your room to show the children how to use the machine.

Management Ideas

When the children are familiar with the listening center routine, they learn quickly to manage the center and are able to handle and return materials independently. However, during the first few weeks of school, the center needs to be checked daily, either before or after school.

> ### Guidelines for Center Users
>
> When children choose to visit the listening center, encourage them to:
>
> 1. Take out only one envelope at a time.
>
> 2. For tape players, rewind the tape when they are finished listening to it.
>
> 3. Return the tape or CD and books to their own envelopes when they are finished listening.

A good way to organize the books and tapes or CDs is to set up a folder system. Staple or tape plain manila folders on each end so that they are open only on the top edge. Print the title of the book on the tab. Remove the title insert from the tape or CD box and glue it to the front of the folder. Place at least two copies of the book and the tape or CD inside the folder.

Daily Maintenance Checklist

☐ Check the contents of the folders to make sure that they contain the proper tapes or CDs and stories.

☐ Check the tapes to be sure that they have been rewound.

☐ Check the condition of books and folders and repair tears and other damage as needed.

Teaching Tips

Start Simple

While it is important to provide choices in all areas of the classroom, offering too many storybook tape or CD sets will only cause confusion during the beginning weeks of school. Start by offering two or three choices and gradually add to that number as time goes by.

Consider Children's Needs

With very young or inexperienced children, the story they have chosen may be longer than their attention span. Children may tire of listening long before the end of the story. Children should be able to end their listening whenever they are ready to do so. It doesn't matter whether the story is finished. The value of the listening experience ceases when the children are no longer able to focus their attention on the story. Insisting that children stay with a story until its conclusion may teach them that listening to stories is a difficult and unpleasant chore. If they have the freedom to listen for as long as their attention span permits and then to move on to another activity, they are more likely to learn that listening is a pleasure. As children mature, their ability to listen will increase.

Model Appropriate Behavior

Some children may not notice or respond to the "turn-the-page" signals when they hear them. Encourage children to experiment for a while. They will usually discover for themselves that turning the page when they hear the signal makes the words and the pictures go together. If a child is becoming frustrated by the story and pictures being out of sync, put on a headset and listen along with the child for awhile. Point out the signal when you hear it, and turn the page of your book. Modeling this behavior will help the child understand what to do to have a successful listening experience.

Assign Peer Tutors

You will find that the listening center will quickly become a completely child-directed center. However, during the introductory period, be sure to make yourself available to those children who need help getting started. Task cards for using the tape recorder will be very useful, but more direct help may also be needed while the children are learning to load the tapes or CDs properly, start the stories, and adjust the headsets. After a few adult-assisted listening experiences, children will be able to manage the physical aspects of the center on their own. As soon as a few children in the class are able to manage the center, putting them to work as peer tutors helping other children get started with the listening equipment makes your job easier and enhances the tutor's self-esteem.

Preview Stories

Choose stories carefully. Consider your class's needs and development level. Children who have not had much experience with books need stories that are short, simple, and fun. Some excellent stories are too long and complicated for younger or inexperienced children. On the other hand, some children will enjoy much more challenging stories. Preview the stories before making them available to children in the center. Consider whether they are appropriate for your children.

Link Listening Experiences to Project Themes

If your class is studying pets, provide story sets that feature cats, dogs, and other household pets. When you place orders through book clubs, be on the lookout for stories and tapes or CDs that will fit into the projects you anticipate for your class in future months. In addition to purchasing your own story tapes and CDs, you can also take advantage of sets available for loan from the public library.

Tips for Success: Remember to . . .

- ☆ Choose stories that will meet the needs of your children.

- ☆ Color code the operating buttons on the equipment.

- ☆ Provide task cards so that children can use the equipment and materials independently.

- ☆ Set up a folder system for storing books and tapes or CDs.

- ☆ Help children get started using the listening equipment appropriately.

- ☆ Model turning the page with the signal, if necessary.

- ☆ Begin collecting storybook sets that will fit into your project themes.

- ☆ Check with your public library for storybook tape or CD sets.

- ☆ Keep tapes, CDs, books, and envelopes in good repair.

Library Center

Children's experiences with books will vary, but most children come to school with some sense of the importance of printed words. The purpose of the library center is to increase that awareness and to instill within the children a love of literature. The books that are provided for children to enjoy should include a broad range of content and format. Children will delight in books with colorful illustrations and will be able to follow a simple story line if it is direct, clear, and meaningful to them. Be sure to choose books that portray diversity in terms of family makeup, culture, ethnicity, and abilities. If you have children who speak languages other than English, make sure that you have books written in the children's home languages. The library center is especially appealing to the child with strong verbal-linguistic intelligence.

Creating a Library Center

The library center works best when it is in a quiet corner of the classroom, as far away from noise as possible. If space is limited in your classroom, you can build a reading loft in your quiet zone by investing in a few materials and a few hours of work. Add wide stairs, secure railings for safety, and carpet on the floor of the loft. This provides a wonderful "hideaway" that is removed from the hustle and bustle of the classroom below.

Essential Materials

Display Cases and Chairs

The library center can also be a small, cozy reading area with space for just a few children to cuddle up with a book. If you choose to create a small, cozy "book nook," equipment needs are simple. You will need a child-size book display case designed with slanting shelves so that a variety of books can be displayed with their covers showing. In order to make the space cozy and inviting, you can easily add softness by putting a laundry basket of throw pillows and stuffed animals on the floor next to the shelf. If space allows, this is also a good place for an adult-sized rocking chair or upholstered chair or loveseat. You can sit with a child on your lap for some one-on-one reading, or a child can share the chair with a friend as they enjoy a good book together.

Quality Picture Books

Fill the book display case with quality picture books. Ask your school librarian or the children's librarian at the public library for a list of recommended books for your classroom library. There are hundreds of appropriate books available. Include in your selection books that have been awarded the Caldecott Medal. The Caldecott is awarded annually to the artist of the best children's picture book, so you can be sure the illustrations will be wonderful. Find a selection of books that will complement the ideas and concepts that you will be teaching. If you contact the children's librarian in advance and discuss the projects you'll be exploring during the month, he or she can help you choose an excellent collection that will ensure a month full of quality children's literature in your classroom.

Try This

Caldecott Medal Winners

2005: *Kitten's First Full Moon,* by Kevin Henkes

2004: *The Man Who Walked Between the Towers,* by Mordicai Gerstein

2003: *My Friend Rabbit,* by Eric Rohmann

2002: *The Three Pigs,* by David Wiesner

2001: *So You Want to Be President?* Illustrated by David Small; Text by Judith St. George

2000: *Joseph Had a Little Overcoat,* by Simms Taback

If space is not a problem, you may choose to set up a larger, more active literacy center that combines the library center with the puppet, listening, writing, ABC, and computer centers. Details on setting up and managing these centers are discussed later in this chapter.

Quiet Corner or "Alone" Spot

Another important feature of the library center is a quiet corner to be used as an "alone" spot for one child to get away from it all. This is especially helpful for the child with what Howard Gardner has called a strong "intrapersonal intelligence," which means she has a strong sense of who she is, and can turn what she knows inside to reflect on herself. The "alone" center might be furnished with something as simple as a large cardboard carton that has been painted or covered with self-adhesive paper and turned upside down. Cut a doorway, add some soft pillows, stuffed animals, and a blanket. Or you can create a quiet corner by covering a small table with a lacy tablecloth or semi-sheer curtains, allowing you to supervise the area while providing a feeling of privacy for the child.

Guidelines for Center Users

When children choose to visit the library center, encourage them to:

1. Turn book pages carefully.

2. Remember that books are for reading, not throwing, standing on, or writing in.

3. Put books away when they finish reading them.

4. Report torn pages and help repair them.

Management Ideas

If the library center is a small, cozy book nook, there are very few management tasks. The center, by its very nature, is a quiet place with little activity. If your library center is large and more active, you will need to check equipment periodically.

> ## Daily Maintenance Checklist
>
> ☐ Make sure the books are displayed attractively and neatly.
>
> ☐ Check the books periodically to see if they are torn or need repair. Remove damaged books until they can be repaired.
>
> ☐ Launder pillows and stuffed animals periodically.
>
> ☐ Have you begun a new theme? If so, change books to complement the new theme.
>

Teaching Tips

Read Books Aloud

The main purpose of the library center is to help children begin to develop a lifelong love of books. To help accomplish this goal, remind children of how special books are by reading quality books to them at least once a day during whole-group storytime. Storytime is an important part of the day in the classroom for young children, and it can become a magical experience for them. Children may ask for a favorite story to be read over and over again. Sometimes they will want to hear it again as soon as you finish reading. That's great! It means that they have fallen in love with the book. Read it as often as they would like to hear it. Before long, some of the children will have the story memorized and they will be able to "read" it to you.

Choose Books Carefully

Be sure that the books you choose to read are written on an appropriate level for your children. Some picture books are too wordy for very young children. If you want to share a book that has more words than your group can handle, show the pictures and tell the story instead of reading it. Talk with the children about the pictures and invite their comments and ideas. Ask them to predict what will happen next and talk about how the characters are feeling.

Practice Good Storytelling Techniques

Get to know the book well before you read it to children. Make sure that you know how to pronounce all of the words and that you understand what they mean. Be certain that you feel comfortable with the story before you share it with children.

If you are reading to the whole class, sit facing the children. Hold the book very still, by the side of your face. Be sure to position the book and yourself in such a way that all the children can see the pages as you read. Practice in front of a mirror until you are comfortable with the technique.

Begin storytime by discussing the book's cover. Tell the children the names of the author and the illustrator. Explain that the author is the person who made up the story and wrote it down and the illustrator drew the pictures. Read the title of the story and ask the children to predict what the story will be about. If the book has a picture on the cover, encourage children to describe what they see.

As you read the story, use your voice to make the story more interesting. If the book's mood is quiet, use a soft, quiet voice. If the book has a lot of action, use your voice to reflect that. If the book is full of suspense, surprise, or drama, use your voice to express those feelings. If the characters in the story talk, choose voices for each character. A bear, for example, might speak in a deep, gruff voice while a bird's voice might be high-pitched and chirpy.

Be Receptive to Children's Reactions

If you begin a story and find that, no matter how hard you try, the children are not interested, choose another story that is more suited to their needs and interests at the moment. There are times when a book you like and have used successfully in the past just doesn't work with a particular group or at a particular time. Be willing to put it away instead of turning storytime into a battle of wills. If you are reading to a group and one child loses interest, allow that child to leave the library center and do something else. This will prevent the child's behavior from interrupting the other children's enjoyment of the story.

Allow some wiggles. It's difficult for young children to sit perfectly still for a long period of time. Expect them to change positions and move around a bit while they are listening. Many children may even be able to concentrate better if they are able to wiggle and move around somewhat. As long as they aren't interfering with anyone else, a little wiggling is fine. Some children might choose to lie down at storytime.

If a child interrupts the story to ask a question or make a comment, you can stop the story and discuss it with the child. If someone is interrupting constantly, however, the story can lose its rhythm and natural flow. When this happens, ask the child to save his or her questions because you would like to talk about them when the story is over. Be sure to follow through and allow discussion at the end of storytime.

Use Volunteer "Book Buddies"

During learning center time, the library center is a place for children to enjoy books on their own. The early childhood days are such a busy time that it can be hard for you to find the time to sit with one or two children and read a book together. Invite parents, senior citizens, and older children to be "book buddies" in the library center. Encourage them to go into the library center and be available to read to the children who choose the center.

Teach Children Proper Book Care

Along with teaching children to enjoy books goes the task of teaching them to take care of books properly. Children who come from homes that are rich in reading opportunities will come to school knowing that books require special care. Other children need to learn that concept at school. The best way to teach children to care for books is to *model appropriate behavior.* Be certain that you always turn pages carefully, return books to the bookshelf, and mend any torn pages you come across. After a little while, the children will come to you to report a torn page. Their response will almost always be, "We need to fix this." Help children get the tape dispenser and fix the damage immediately. Praise their efforts and let them know how glad you are that they care about books.

 ## Tips for Success: Remember to . . .

☆ Display books attractively.

☆ Find volunteers who can read informally to children during learning center time.

☆ Practice good reading techniques in front of a mirror.

☆ Get to know the story before you read it to the children.

☆ Tell children about authors, illustrators, and dedications.

☆ Stop the story when the children have lost interest.

☆ Tell stories that are too difficult to read to young children.

☆ Allow for some interruptions, questions, and comments about the story.

☆ Expect wiggles during storytime.

☆ Invite children to help repair broken books and torn pages.

☆ Use your voice to convey the mood of the story.

Writing Center

The writing center is, as its name implies, a place where children have opportunities to develop writing skills. Writing is an important part of literacy development and should be available to children every day as one of the free-choice learning center activities. While most children in an early childhood program are not ready for a great deal of formal writing instruction, they can benefit from a variety of experiences that emphasize the importance of letters, signs, and symbols.

Creating a Writing Center

The writing center does not need to be large or elaborate. It may be a small center in a quiet area of the classroom or it may be a part of the library center. The only furniture needed for a writing center is a table and several chairs. Stock the area with different types and sizes of paper such as copier paper, tablets, note pads, and stationery. You can also create simple booklets by stapling several sheets of paper together with a wraparound cover made from wallpaper samples or construction paper to encourage children to become authors.

Essential Materials

A variety of writing tools should be available in the writing center, such as pencils, ballpoint pens, felt-tip pens, colored pens, colored pencils, markers, and crayons. You might also want to include letter and numeral stencils or alphabet stamps with stamp pads. Hang an alphabet chart on the wall at the children's eye level. Provide picture dictionaries and word books. One way to encourage written communication among children in the class is to provide a mailbox for each child. You can make a class set of mailboxes by cutting the tops off of half-gallon milk cartons, turning them on their sides, and taping or gluing them together. Label cartons with names and photographs of the people in the classroom, including teachers. Cover the set with self-adhesive plastic so that it will be sturdy and attractive and place it in or near the writing center.

Try This

The Power of Two

Combine your writing center with the computer center so that children can have the experience of entering data and printing out their results.

Name Writing

Many four- and five-year-old children become interested in writing their names as well as their classmates' names. When you notice this interest developing in your classroom, take advantage of the teaching opportunity by making a name card for each child. Start by using a colored marker to print each name on an index card or sentence strip in model manuscript printing. Next, carefully trace over each letter with white glue, colored glue, or glitter glue. After the glue dries, trace the letters with glue one more time so they become significantly raised from the surface. This gives children the opportunity to both see and feel the shapes of the letters in their names. Some additional ways to provide three-dimensional name cards are to cut the letters out of sandpaper or form them out of yarn and glue them to cards or sentence strips.

Keep in Mind

Touchable Names

The tactile aspect of name cards helps the children understand the nature of letters.

Theme-Related Materials

To keep the center interesting, provide materials that relate to your project themes of study. For example, if your class is studying farm animals, post some pictures of farm animals with their names printed on the pictures. Add a box of sentence strips or index cards on which you have written animal names and glued plastic toy animals. If you are going to visit a farm, invite the children to write lists of the animals they want to see. After the visit, encourage the children to write thank-you notes to the farmer and stories about the trip. If you keep literacy development in mind at all times, you will be able to find many ways to add writing opportunities to all of your units of study throughout the year.

Management Ideas

The writing center is usually a very popular center, so materials are used up at a rapid rate. Be sure an adequate supply of writing materials is available at all times.

Guidelines for Center Users

When children choose to visit the writing center, encourage them to:

❶ Write only on their own paper (unless children have agreed to collaborate on a writing project).

❷ Replace caps on markers.

❸ Return pens and pencils to their proper places.

Daily Maintenance Checklist

☐ Replenish paper supply as needed.

☐ Sharpen pencils and discard and replace worn-out pens and markers.

☐ Replenish the supply of teacher-made blank books as needed.

☐ If you are using a stamp pad, replenish the ink as needed.

Teaching Tips

Respect Developmental Stages

Young children go through predictable stages in the development of their writing. It is important to understand that each stage is normal and necessary so you can facilitate learning and avoid trying to teach children to write before they are ready.

One of the first stages of writing is **scribbling**. A child in this stage may fill page after page with scribbles. Respect the child's attempts and show interest in the work without correcting, criticizing, or trying to improve on it. After scribbling, children typically move into a period of *mock letter formation*. They aren't quite making letters correctly, but their scribbles look more similar to conventional writing. Again, there may be pages and pages of mock letters during this stage. The mock letter stage is followed by *actual letters written in random fashion* with no relationship to the sounds they represent. Letters used in this stage are often letters found in the child's name since that is the single most important word in the child's life and is usually the first word a child can read. A child in this stage might write the letters k, p, a, t, s and read it as "We went to the zoo."

Keep in Mind

Let Them Stand Uncorrected

Accept what children write and read without correction.

Eventually children will begin making some connections between letters and sounds. When this happens, *invented spelling* begins showing up in writing. This might begin with writing one letter to represent a word, but the letter has some relationship to the sounds in the word. As children mature, their invented spelling progresses into *actual spelling* when you will be able to read much of the writing without needing the child's interpretation. The age at which this level of sophistication in writing emerges varies from child to child. Ages may range from four years to six or seven years and still be considered perfectly normal development.

Understanding the stages of writing can help you support children's literacy development. Accept children's beginning efforts. Express an interest in children's ideas without criticism or correction. Trust that literacy is emerging as it should and according to each child's own individual "blueprint" for development.

Mix of mock and real letters (4-year-old)

Original message conveying a complete thought—"I made puzzles." (4-year-old)

Short letter—"Mr. Flag, the swing is broken." (4-year-old)

Original short story—"Bell is drinking the grape juice. She is sharing with her boyfriends, she says." (5-year-old)

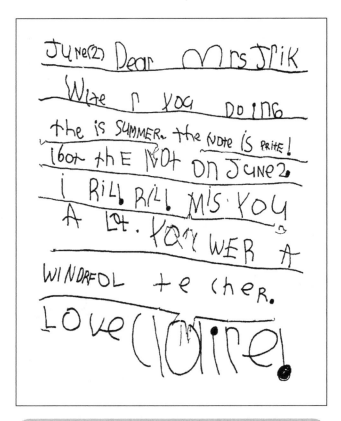

Complex letter that conveys many thoughts—"June (2) Dear Mrs. Jurek, What are you doing this summer? The note is pretty. I got the note on June 2. I really really miss you a lot. You were a wonderful teacher. Love, Claire." (6-year-old)

Listen to Children "Read" Their Writing

Build time into your daily schedule to listen to children "read" their writing. You might have a few minutes at storytime when an author sits in a special chair and reads an original story to the class. I call this *VIP Reader Time.* When you establish this as a daily routine, you'll find that so many children want a turn at being a VIP Reader that you'll have to establish a waiting list—another literacy opportunity!

You can also encourage writing on an individual level by visiting the writing center or library center from time to time to listen to a child read privately to you. Ask leading questions when a story is in progress, such as, "What is going to happen next?" or "How did she feel when that happened?"

Make Positive and Supportive Comments

Make positive, supportive comments when you see connections between oral and written language. For example, if a child writes the letter h and reads it as "horse," comment on the relationship between the letter and the initial sound of the word. Phonemic awareness is a critical part of reading readiness, so celebrate milestones like this with your children!

Model the Usefulness of Writing

Sit at the writing center from time to time, write notes to children, and put them in their mailboxes. You also want children to see you writing notes to parents or other staff members about daily needs or information. If you need for the custodian to leave a fresh roll of paper towels for the next day, make a show of writing a note and post it where it can been seen. Discuss your writing and its purpose with children. Emphasize the letters you are using and the sounds they represent and read your notes aloud. Encourage other adults to write letters to your class. Reading the letters and posting them on the wall in the writing center along with children's writing helps children see the value of writing.

Encourage Children's Writing

Invite children to write about their daily matters and concerns. For example, keep a shopping list posted on the wall or in a special folder in the writing center. When you run out of red paint in the art center, ask a child to add red paint to the shopping list. If a child notices that a swing is broken on the playground, ask that child to write a note to the custodian about the broken equipment. If a child is sick, encourage the children to write get well notes to the child. Collect the notes, put them in an envelope, and actually mail them to the sick child's home.

Try This

Start a Pen Pal Club With Another Class

Take snapshots of each child and include the snapshots with the first letters your class writes to the pen pal class.

When you start looking for ways to encourage children's writing, you will find that each and every day brings with it many opportunities for children to use written language in a meaningful way.

Tips for Success: Remember to . . .

- ✪ Keep a fresh supply of paper, blank books, and writing materials on hand.

- ✪ Be aware of the different stages of writing development.

- ✪ Encourage children to write notes, shopping lists, and reminders.

- ✪ Accept each child's writing at his or her own level, without correction or criticism.

- ✪ Listen to children as they read what they have written.

- ✪ Model writing.

- ✪ Provide mailboxes for everyone in the class and use them for messages.

- ✪ Think of ways to relate meaningful writing experiences to your units of study.

ABC Center

The ABC Center focuses attention on the alphabet. Research has shown that readiness for reading requires that children be familiar with the alphabet. One way to ensure that this happens during the preschool and kindergarten years is to provide an "ABC Center."

Creating an ABC Center

Essential Materials

This center can be very simple. All you really need is a low, open shelf, labeled with words and pictures to represent the items stored on the shelves. You can position the shelf next to your writing center table or, if space allows, you can provide a table and chairs specifically for the ABC Center. The ABC Center and the Writing Center go hand-in-hand, with a lot of interaction between the two areas.

Items for the ABC Center include

alphabet books

alphabet puzzles

magnetic letters with magnetic boards

alphabet stencils and stamps

teacher-made alphabet games

tactile letters

alphabet charts

A "letter wall" or a "word wall" will fit well into the ABC Center. Post large letters of the alphabet and/or frequently used words the children know on the wall in this center. Try to place them low enough for the children to touch them and trace the letters with their fingers.

Keep in Mind

Material Upkeep

If you provide stamps and stencils, be sure that there is an ample supply of paper and that the stamp pads are in good condition.

Management Ideas

As with other centers, the key to management is organization. Make sure that your shelves and containers are labeled clearly with pictures and words, using English and the children's home languages, if possible, for your

Guidelines for Center Users

When children visit the ABC Center, encourage them to:

❶ Choose only one alphabet set at a time.

❷ Work with their alphabet materials on trays.

❸ Use stamps and stencils only on their own paper, unless two or more children have agreed to work cooperatively on a shared project.

❹ Return materials to their labeled places on the shelf.

labeling. Check your containers from time to time to ensure that all of the the letters are present. If letters are missing, remove the set from the center until you can replace the missing letter or letters. It can be very frustrating for a child who is looking for a "J" to finish a story and the "J" is nowhere to be found!

Cafeteria trays can help keep alphabet sets together. Life in the early childhood classroom is much less complicated if the magnetic letters, the sponge letters, and the rubber letters stay in their own containers instead of getting mixed up together, causing confusion and frustration.

Daily Maintenance Checklist

☐ Check alphabet sets to make sure that each set is complete and in its own labeled container.

☐ Remove any sets with missing letters.

☐ Check the paper supply and replenish as needed.

☐ Check stamp pads and replenish ink as needed.

Teaching Tips

Provide "Forgiving" Materials

Workbook pages that focus on writing or tracing letters can be laminated and placed in this center along with dry erase markers and erasers. Children can then practice their alphabet skills, erase their marks, and do it again. These kinds of "forgiving" materials are especially helpful for children who have difficulty forming letters or getting the "right" answers for activities that require alphabet knowledge. There are no papers marked with wrong answers for all the world to see. The child can simply erase the mistakes and try again!

Stop By and Stay a While

Informal visits with children as they use the ABC Center can be very helpful to you in terms of assessing skills, abilities, and needs. You can also help the children learn the "right answer" by talking with them about their work, providing a scaffold for their learning. Alphabet knowledge is something that children learn from others, so be ready to spend some time in this area, sharing your knowledge and helping children build their skills.

Encourage Peer Tutoring

The ABC Center is a good place to promote peer tutoring. If you have a child who already knows the names and sounds of most of the letters in the alphabet, encourage the other children to go to the "alphabet expert" when they need help. This is a win-win situation. The child who needs help gets what is needed. The child who provides the tutoring has an opportunity to reinforce existing skills and to have a self-esteem enhancing experience. And the teacher is free to move about the room, taking advantage of other "teachable moments," with the knowledge that the ABC Center is in good hands.

A B C Tips for Success: Remember to . . .

☆ Provide labeled containers or trays for each alphabet set

☆ Provide a labeled place for each item on the shelf

✭ Spend time informally talking with children and teaching them about letter names, shapes and sound relationships

✭ Laminate workbook-type pages, making them forgivable

✭ Encourage peer tutoring

Computer Center

Computers are now a common household item for many families, but even for children who've never used or even seen one before entering your class, computers are excellent learning tools. Children learn about cause and effect when they punch a key on the keyboard and see the results on the monitor. By playing with computers and talking with other children and adults about their play, children develop awareness of letters and numerals. Software is available to provide children with opportunities to practice many varied skills and to test themselves on a variety of concepts.

Creating a Computer Center

While the computer center can stand alone, it fits in nicely with the other literacy centers. Children can move seamlessly from books to writing to printing stories on the computer's printer if they are all in the same general area.

Essential Materials

Your class needs a basic computer, easy access to electricity, a monitor, color printer, a table or child-sized computer desk to contain the equipment, age-appropriate software, and a low, accessible place to store software and paper. A scanner is a nice addition but not a necessity. Keep plain white computer paper in great abundance, and add colored paper from time to time to keep interest high.

Provide at least two child-size chairs in your computer center. Children benefit most from using computers if they can interact with at least one other child in the process. They share ideas and information and learn from one another when they can work together on computer projects.

Keep in Mind

Safety at All Times

Be sure that electrical supply cords are safely out of the traffic areas to avoid tripping hazards!

Management Ideas

If you have children who aren't familiar with computers, they'll need some instruction and guidance at the beginning of the school year regarding the way the equipment works and how to properly care for it. Task cards and color-coding can be helpful in teaching children how to turn the computer on and off, how to select programs, and how to save their work to a disk.

Depending upon your students' computer experience levels, you may want to begin the school year with only preloaded programs. Make sure that you have a simple word processing program so that children can use the computer for "writing" from the very beginning of the year. As they become more computer literate, you can add software, one or two new programs at a time, along with task card directions for opening and using the programs.

Guidelines for Center Users

When children choose to visit the computer center, encourage them to:

❶ Use gentle touches with the keyboard and other equipment.

❷ Load disks properly.

❸ Replace software in its proper place when they finish using it.

❹ Place printouts in the appropriate place.

You'll want to decide what to do with computer printouts that children create. Children might place them in their cubbies to take home, or you might have a special basket or tote tray where works in progress can be stored at the end of the day, ready to be revisited at another time. Be sure that children sign or print their names on their work so that ownership can be easily determined.

Daily Maintenance Checklist

☐ Make sure that software is in its appropriate place.

☐ Turn the computer off at the end of the day.

☐ Check the printer's paper supply and replenish as needed.

☐ Check the printer's ink supply and replace or refill cartridges as needed.

Teaching Tips

Choose Appropriate Software

There are thousands of computer products available to teachers of young children, with new ones being developed daily. When you are selecting software, shop wisely, keeping your children's needs, interests, and developmental levels in mind. It might help to ask yourself three questions:

❶ What skills or concepts will the children gain through using this software?

❷ Is this program going to match my children's skills, abilities, and levels of understanding?

❸ Does this software allow the children to explore, experiment, and solve problems?

Software that offers *varying of levels of difficulty* within one program enables the less mature child to succeed while challenging the more advanced learner. Flexibility and variety, along with age-appropriateness and opportunities for action and problem solving, are keys to selecting software that will be beneficial for your children.

Join in the Action

Stop by the Computer Center from time to time to talk with the children who are using the equipment. Ask them about their activities and show interest in their discoveries and skills. This will give you insight into their progress and help you plan for future software purchases. If you have a child who has written a story and wants help keying it into the computer, lend a hand. You might do the typing yourself or, better yet, help the child find the appropriate keys. Comparing the shapes of letters in different fonts can be an interesting topic of conversation and may lead to an entire project for your class.

Be Brave

Sometimes children are more comfortable with computers than their teachers are! That's because they see it as a toy, not a threat. If you consider yourself "low tech" and are uncomfortable with computers, relax. Have fun and learn about the computer alongside the children. Most new computers are very user-friendly. They come equipped with cute little wizards and other cartoon-type figures to help guide you when you're unsure of what to do next. If you approach computers like the children do—as an interesting new toy to explore—you'll find yourself developing new skills and confidence every day!

Tips for Success: Remember to . . .

- ✪ Select software that fits your children's ages and stages of development and interests
- ✪ Set up spaces for at least two children to use the computer at the same time
- ✪ Join in and participate with the children in their computer activities

8

Math and Manipulatives Center

At the math and manipulatives center, children work with puzzles and string beads, make patterns with geoboards, play matching and sorting games, stack cylinders, and much more. The puzzles, matching games, and other materials are all designed to teach specific skills such as recognizing shapes, sizes, numbers, colors, and likenesses and differences; counting; sequencing; and ordering. Because many mathematical concepts are best learned using manipulative materials, this area is often called a "math and manipulatives center." Children also develop eye-hand coordination and practice using the small muscles in their hands and fingers when they work with manipulative materials.

Creating a Manipulative Center

The manipulative center is one of the easiest to position in the room. It doesn't have any special requirements in terms of water, electricity, or floor covering. It can also serve as a buffer between your active and quiet areas in the dry zone.

Essential Materials

The essentials for this center include low, open bookcases and a box of carpet squares or cafeteria trays. You can purchase carpet squares for a very reasonable price, or you may be able to get a local carpet store to donate discontinued samples. Cafeteria trays are an alternative to carpet squares. They work just as well and are readily available from food suppliers or perhaps from your own school cafeteria.

Carpet Squares and Trays

The children use carpet squares or trays to help define the space for their work. For example, a child working a puzzle can keep all of the pieces on one carpet square. This will help keep the pieces from different puzzles from getting mixed together into a confusing, frustrating jumble. Young children are usually very comfortable working on the floor, and they enjoy having the space the floor provides to spread out while they work. If space is abundant in your classroom, you might want to add a table and chairs in the manipulative center. If you choose to have a table and chairs, the carpet squares and trays will still be important. Encourage children to use them on the table instead of the floor.

Keep in Mind

Children's Spatial Preferences

Young children are usually very comfortable working on the floor, and they enjoy having the space the floor provides to spread out while they work.

Materials for Different Stages of Development

When you're choosing materials to equip the center, think about the skills your children already have and the ones you want them to develop. Some children will begin school with a lot of experience with puzzles and other manipulative materials, and they will be ready for more challenging activities. For example, some four-year-olds are ready at the beginning of the school year for a fifteen-piece puzzle. Other children will come to school with very little experience with these types of materials. For these children, provide very simple activities, such as one- or two-piece puzzles. Providing a range of activities to meet the needs of children at both ends of the experience spectrum helps ensure that all of the children are successful and are challenged.

As the name of the center implies, the math and manipulatives center is a natural hub of activity revolving around mathematical thinking. Provide plenty of materials and opportunities for children to count, sort, seriate, order, and group objects, thus developing their emerging mathematical-thinking skills. Many simple materials such as a deck of cards and a set of dominoes go a long way to enhance the development of these skills in this center.

Homemade Materials

School supply catalogs and teacher stores are full of well-made, interesting, and developmentally appropriate materials for the manipulative center. It is possible to purchase virtually everything you need for this center. However, this approach can become very expensive. Take heart, though: some of the best manipulative materials can be homemade.

Using the same concept, you can transform almost all worksheet and workbook pages into developmentally appropriate manipulative activities at very little cost.

You can also use *coloring books* to make manipulative materials. Color a picture, mount it on a piece of tagboard, laminate it, and cut it into several puzzle pieces. Invite children to match the pieces to complete the whole picture. For less mature children or with a more complicated puzzle, you might want to use two identical pictures and leave one picture whole for children to use as a reference guide.

Shelves

Low, open, easy-to-reach shelves are a necessity in the manipulatives center. Each activity needs its own self-contained box, basket, or tray, located on its own special place on the shelf. You can make the materials look attractive and inviting by covering boxes with colorful self-adhesive plastic and using a permanent marker to write the

Try This

Making Manipulatives

Turn activity sheets from workbooks and worksheets into hands-on manipulative activities. A worksheet may have a variety of pictures of hot and cold objects and direct children to draw an X on each cold object. To turn this into a manipulative activity, color the pictures on the worksheet, glue the sheet to a piece of tagboard, cut the pictures out, and laminate them. Place the laminated pictures in a press-to-seal plastic bag. On one side of a manila file folder write "Cold" and glue a picture of something cold next to it. On the other side write "Hot" and glue a picture of something hot next to it. Place the plastic bag of pictures in the folder and place the folder activity on a shelf in the manipulative center. When children choose the file folder activity, they can place the pictures under the correct heading.

activity name on the outside of the box. A puzzle rack for stacking several wooden inlay puzzles is nice to have but not absolutely essential. You do, however, want to avoid stacking puzzles on top of each other. If you don't have a puzzle rack, just place the puzzles side by side on the shelves.

Management Ideas

The manipulative center is one of the easiest-to-manage centers in the classroom. If it has been set up carefully, it virtually maintains itself.

Puzzles

To help prevent confusion with mixed-up puzzle pieces, write a number on the back of each puzzle piece. For example, write the number "1" on the back of each piece from the tiger puzzle and the number "2" on the back of each piece from the elephant puzzle. If there is an accidental mix-up, it is easier to separate the pieces.

Wooden inlay puzzles don't have to be thrown out if a piece is lost. To repair the puzzle, purchase a can of wood filler at a hardware store. Wood filler is a paste that dries to a wood-like consistency. Assemble the puzzle with the pieces that are still available. Coat the space for the missing piece with petroleum jelly, including the sides of the adjacent pieces. Fill in the space with the wood filler and allow it to dry. Remove the new pieces and smooth any rough spots with sandpaper. Paint the pieces as needed. Clean off the excess petroleum jelly from the puzzle base. The puzzle is repaired and ready for action again!

Guidelines for Center Users

When children visit the manipulative center, encourage them to:

❶ Put their work on carpet squares or cafeteria trays.

❷ Complete puzzles before returning them to the shelf. (If they cannot complete it themselves, have them invite a friend to help.)

❸ Return all pieces of an activity to the basket or tray and replace it on the shelf when they are finished.

Daily Maintenance Checklist

☐ Make sure everything is in order on the shelves, with all pieces in place.

☐ Add additional materials if children need more challenging activities.

☐ Look over materials for missing pieces. If a piece has been lost and you can't find it, take the activity out of the center and put it away until it can be repaired.

Teaching Tips

Ask Open-Ended Questions

Ask open-ended questions to extend the children's learning while they work with manipulative materials. For question suggestions, refer to Bloom's Taxonomy on page 23.

Encourage Children to Be Problem Solvers

When children begin a new activity, invite them to "read" the directions on the task card with you. Encourage them to show you how to do the activity. Remember that the best teaching is usually done by asking, not telling. Explore the activity with the children and ask them how they think it might work. Encourage them to try it out and see for themselves if they are on the right track. If the first attempt is unsuccessful, suggest that children think of another way to do it. When you see that the children understand the directions and know how to work with the materials, stand back. Remember that your goal is to teach children to think and solve problems for themselves instead of giving them the answers and solutions.

Encourage Children to Help Each Other

If a child is having trouble with a puzzle that's new or too difficult, try to avoid the temptation of doing it for the child or showing how it is to be done. Instead, suggest that the child ask a friend for help. There is usually a "puzzle expert" in every class. Encourage the child who needs help to ask the friend to come over and lend a hand. This is a terrific way to build the "expert's" self-esteem, and it helps the other children see that each person has his or her own unique strengths and abilities. Children can learn much from each other if you give them a chance to be a teacher themselves from time to time.

Tips for Success: Remember to . . .

- ✿ Observe the children while they work and look for demonstration of skills that have been mastered.

- ✿ Provide carpet squares or cafeteria trays where the children can easily reach them.

- ✿ Remind the children, if necessary, about working on the carpet squares or cafeteria trays.

- ✿ Check the materials daily and remove anything with missing pieces.

- ✿ Show an interest in children's discoveries.

- ✿ Talk with the children about their work and ask open-ended questions.

- ✿ Encourage a child who is having difficulty to ask a friend for help.

- ✿ Remind the children to return an activity to the shelf before choosing another one.

- ✿ Make sure that every activity is self-contained in a basket, tray, or box.

- ✿ Include task card directions for all activities.

- ✿ Encourage children to read the directions for information.

9

Science Center

The science center is an exciting place for mixing, manipulating, and experimenting, and for exploring the world. This center could also be called the *discovery center* because discovery is what science is all about. In the science center, children have the opportunity to use all of their senses as they explore nature and basic scientific principles. They learn about geology as they examine, compare, and experiment with different kinds of rocks. They're exposed to chemistry by mixing different substances together and watching the results. The basics of botany are found in this center when the children plant seeds, water them, and watch plants sprout, grow, and change. Biology is introduced in the science center when the children use their sense of smell to match substances in jars and use their sense of touch to describe the objects inside a bag or box.

Caring for pets, hatching eggs, and observing animals are some ways the children learn about zoology. Entomology is a favorite subject for many children who enjoy collecting insects, watching an ant farm, and observing the life cycle of a butterfly. Physics is introduced through experimentation with simple machines like pulleys and levers. The science center is an active, lively place that is full of change and opportunities for wonder! It is especially appealing and helpful to children whose stronger intelligences are naturalist and logical-mathematical.

Creating a Science Center

If possible, place your science center in an area that is near both windows and electrical outlets. If it is not possible to have both, choose a location near a window. Many science activities require sunlight and opportunities to look outside to observe weather conditions. If you are in a classroom with no windows, hang two "grow lights" on either side of the center to aid plant growth.

Essential Materials

Table

Arrange a child-size table and enough chairs for the number of children who will use the center at one time. If your room is small and won't accommodate a large table, use a small table for the "messy" activities. The children can do other science activities on the floor using carpet squares as work mats. Ideally, the science center will be located in your messy zone, because messy activities and spills are to be expected. A tile floor is much easier to maintain!

Shelves

Low, open shelves are another necessary ingredient of the science center. This is where you'll house the science activities. To provide enough variety and interest in the center, try to plan for about two and one-half activities for each child using the center at one time. For example, if the center can accommodate six children, fifteen activities should be available. The center is easiest to manage if you place all of the necessary materials for each activity in its own labeled container or on a tray. When the children enter the center, they can go to the shelf, choose their activities, take them to the work table or designated area, and then clean up and return the materials to the shelf before they choose another activity. For more information on task cards, see "Task Cards" on page 168.

Keep in Mind

Developing Other Skills

Task cards in the containers or on the trays allow the activities to be self-directed, and provide meaningful experiences in literacy.

Another way to add interest and encourage literacy skills is to add a book display shelf filled with science and nature magazines and picture books. Children enjoy browsing through the books and magazines and discussing their discoveries with the other children in the center.

Other Assorted Items

Include safe, nontoxic indoor plants in the science center as well as magnets, magnifying glasses, balance scales, kaleidoscopes, thermometers, rocks, shells, and insect cages.

Classroom Pets

The science center can be a great home for classroom pets. Guinea pigs make wonderful classroom pets because they are usually very even-tempered and will accept a lot of touching and handling without getting nervous or trying to escape. They are big enough for children to hold easily, slow enough to catch if they begin to wander away, and relatively easy to find if they escape. They're fun to have in the classroom because they squeak and whistle when children sing and talk to them. They also love being hand-fed carrots, apples, and other crunchy raw fruits and vegetables. Rabbits are almost as much fun as guinea pigs, but they tend to be a bit more high strung and could scratch if picked up suddenly. But most of the time, it's safe to let a rabbit hop about in the classroom.

Keep in Mind

Nibbling Rabbits

One major drawback to having a free-roaming rabbit is that it will nibble on everything it sees, including extension cords and other classroom materials.

Other pets to consider include gerbils, hamsters, rats, and mice. Smaller animals are less messy, but they can't be handled as freely as bigger ones. They are much more likely to escape and get lost, which can create quite a distraction in your classroom and, perhaps, throughout the whole school. Birds, fish, snakes, land hermit crabs, and lizards can also be great classroom pets.

Always check with your local health department before purchasing a pet. Some regulatory agencies have limitations on the types of animals that are allowed in classrooms and under what conditions the children may interact with them.

It is also important to consider your own comfort level when choosing a pet. If you are squeamish about reptiles or rodents, don't have them in your classroom. You need to be able to enjoy holding and handling the pets in order to provide a good role model for the children.

Management Ideas

The amount of preparation needed in the science center will vary with the activities you have planned. Some science activities are quite messy and complicated and will take up a lot of your preparation time. Others are simple and only require a quick checkup. If you have an ambitious project planned in the art center or in another area of the room, keep the science activities simple to help maintain your sanity. Too many complicated projects at once make the classroom very difficult to manage.

Maintenance

If you choose to have a classroom pet, cleaning cages or litter boxes must become part of your daily routine. Cages will give off an unpleasant odor if they are not cleaned every day. Again, check with your health department for restrictions regarding children's involvement in pet care. In some areas, children are not allowed to help with cage cleaning.

Make "care signs" to make daily routines such as feeding pets and watering plants easy to manage. Use clothespins to attach appropriate signs to plant pots and pet cages. When the jobs have been done, the children turn the sign to the happy face side. This not only provides an opportunity for children to use print in a meaningful way, but it also tells the other children that the jobs have been done. This will prevent your plants from being over-watered and the pets from being overfed. Remember to use the children's home languages, when possible, as well as English for your signs.

To prevent your plants from being overwatered, provide small spray bottles of water instead of watering cans. It is much more difficult to overspray than it is to tip a watering can up until it is emptied. You can buy spray bottles in the garden department of your supermarket, or you can improvise with clean, empty pump spray bottles. If you use the latter, be sure to cover them with decorative self-adhesive vinyl so that children don't get the mistaken idea that hair spray or whatever was originally in the bottle is good for plants.

Try This

Have the Plants Been Watered?

On a large index card, write "The plants have been watered" along with a happy face. On the other side of the card write, "The plants have not been watered" along with a frowning face.

Guidelines for Center Users

When children choose to visit the science center, encourage them to:

❶ Follow the task cards and use materials and equipment for their intended purpose.

❷ Clean up after themselves.

❸ Put things back where they found them. This includes returning all the parts of an activity to its basket or tray and replacing it on the shelf.

❹ Handle pets and other living things gently.

You may need to add special limits that are appropriate for specific activities. If, for example, you have an activity that involves electrical appliances, place a "Do Not Touch" sign on the appliance. Block off an area on the table with red tape that indicates that this space is only for adult hands.

Daily Maintenance Checklist

☐ Check the activities on the shelf to make sure that all the parts and pieces are in good condition and ready for use.

☐ Cover the table with newspapers if a messy activity is planned. Turn the "care signs" around on the pets and plants.

☐ Replenish pet food supply.

☐ Refill plant watering bottles.

☐ Replenish other materials as needed.

☐ Check the center for any additional clean-up needs.

Teaching Tips

Closely Supervise Pet Care

When children care for pets, they need close supervision. If they are allowed to clean cages, help them do so carefully, putting down fresh bedding materials and providing fresh food and water for the pet. If your pet is one that can be handled, encourage children to touch and play with the pet in a gentle manner. The most likely times that pets may bite are when the pets are being removed from or returned to their cages. Consequently, it is usually best for an adult to do this job. Teach the children through your example and by your words how to hold the pets properly so that everyone will enjoy a safe, pleasant experience.

Monitor Science Experiments

Some science activities may involve the use of heat, electricity, and/or tools. Closely monitor these experiments and never permit children to do them unattended. If you or another adult are going to be assigned to the science center for supervision, make sure the activities at other centers are self-managing that day. When the activity is completed, remove equipment to a safe place where children cannot reach it and use it unsupervised.

Introduce Activities to the Whole Group

Many science experiences will have a sequence of steps to follow. Planting seeds, for example, requires that each step be done in sequential order. Prepare task cards to communicate each step to children. Morning Meeting is a great time to introduce these types of activities to the whole group. Read through the task card directions with the children and ask them to help demonstrate the steps involved. This will ensure that all of the children understand the activity and will be able to follow the directions independently and successfully when they go to the center.

Talk With Children About Their Discoveries

As the children work in the science center, stop to talk with them about their discoveries. Ask them to tell you about their

Try This

Inquiry-Based Learning

If children are doing a sink and float activity with various objects and a tub of water, ask questions such as

- "What would happen if the cork were bigger?"
- "What would happen if the wooden block was blue instead of red?"
- "Would the cup sink if you put the spoon in it? Why or why not?"

observations. Ask about textures, tastes, smells, and changes they have experienced. Help them recall the steps they followed and what happened first, second, and so on. Open-ended questions are great teaching tools in the science center. In fact, *questioning is one of your most important jobs in the science center.* Ask questions that will challenge students to think.

Challenge yourself to create questions that will lead the children into further exploration and discovery learning. For more question suggestions, see Bloom's Taxonomy on page 23.

Be a Facilitator

The goal in the science center is to create a rich and interesting environment that will lead children into making discoveries on their own. Don't be tempted to give children too much information. It is much more important for them to discover the information for themselves. Instead of being a dispenser of knowledge, think of yourself as a facilitator of learning. Set up stimulating environments, create challenges so that children can construct their own knowledge through their experiments and explorations, and step back to watch the discovery process happen.

 ## Tips for Success: Remember to . . .

- ☆ Plan and prepare the environment so that everything has a place and a clear purpose.

- ☆ Plan and prepare for mess management.

- ☆ Plan and prepare for activities that involve potentially dangerous equipment by creating a "Do Not Touch" zone with red tape and a sign.

☆ Make sure that an adult is in the science center—at all times—when potentially dangerous materials and equipment are being used.

☆ Make sure that all materials and equipment are ready before school starts.

☆ Supervise and assist, as needed, with plant and pet care.

☆ Ask open-ended questions while the children explore.

☆ Show a sincere interest in the children's discoveries.

☆ Allow the children to do the activities themselves, even if it would be easier and faster to do some of the steps yourself.

10

Music Center

The last of the seven basic centers is the music center—where children experiment with sounds, rhythm, music, and movement. Even if you are in a school that is fortunate enough to have a special music teacher, you still need a music center. Going to a music class once or twice a week isn't enough to meet the children's needs!

Creating a Music Center

The music center is a noisy, active, energetic center and belongs in the active area, as far as possible from the quiet areas. The music center requires a fairly large, open area so that the children have enough space to dance and move creatively. An electrical outlet is important for the music center because you will need to plug in CD and/or tape players. Remember to keep power cords secured and out of the way to avoid tripping hazards, and battery compartments securely closed to avoid loose batteries in the environment.

Essential Materials

Musical Instruments

A piano is a great addition, but you can have a very effective music center without one. One instrument you may want to include is the autoharp. The autoharp is a wonderfully easy-to-use, old-fashioned instrument that both adults and very young children can play successfully. You can learn to play the autoharp with very little effort, even if you have had no musical training. Most autoharps come with a pick, but picks tend to be too small for children's hands to control. A sturdy feather or a small plastic spatula helps children strum the autoharp strings and produce a pleasant sound.

Most school supply catalogs have rhythm band sets that consist of high-quality instruments that will last through years of classroom use. Give some consideration, however, to the types of rhythm instruments that you provide in the center for free exploration. If you have a high tolerance for noise, you might be comfortable with cymbals and drums being available every day as a free choice instrument. If not, you may want to put some instruments away during learning center time and use them only for group music experiences. Too much noise in a classroom creates a stressful environment for everyone—children and adults alike. So don't feel badly if you decide to save the louder instruments for more controlled situations.

CD and Tape Players

Young children can learn to operate CD and tape players independently. Little hands can be rough on electronic equipment, however, so the equipment may not last as long as it would with adult-only use. If you go to a flea market or garage sale and pick up used (but working) CD and tape players, you can relax and allow the children to experience independence without worrying about the cost of replacing expensive equipment. Do the same with tapes and CDs. If you purchase used CDs that already have a scratch or two, little harm is done when they are loaded upside down or backwards into the player, and inexpensive CD "repair kits" are available from music and discount stores. Task card directions are helpful to teach children the proper way to use CD and tape players. Placing the directions on the wall near the equipment makes it easy for the children to see and follow.

You might also want to designate one CD or tape player as an "adult only" piece of equipment. You can place this one out of reach of the children along with a supply of good tapes and CDs. This "yours" and "mine" approach allows the children the freedom and independence they need, enables you to provide beautiful music for your classroom, and keeps you from getting upset about your favorite tape or CD being ruined.

Song Book

Another useful addition to the music center is a book with your class's favorite songs written out with both words and pictures of the words. This helps inspire the children's spontaneous singing, and it is a great way to promote literacy. The children begin to associate the written word with the words they are singing and are soon able to "read" the songs. *You* don't have to be a great "musical artist" to do this. Just think of the songs your class enjoys and write them down with as many pictures as you can. Stick figures will do just fine, or you can use pictures you cut out of coloring books. Laminate them for durability.

Movement Props

You'll want to collect a variety of movement props such as hats and scarves for children to use as they express music with their bodies. Be on the lookout for high schools that are getting new band uniforms and talk with the director about donating some of the old uniforms and hats to your class.

Guidelines for Center Users

When children visit the music center, encourage them to:

1 Follow the task card directions, and use the instruments properly.

2 Take out only one tape or CD at a time.

3 Return the instruments, tapes, CDs, and other materials to their proper places when they are finished using them.

Management Ideas

Each instrument and movement prop needs its own space and its own container. For example, you might have a variety of scarves for creative movement. Placing the scarves in a box or basket labeled with a sign that has a picture of scarves and the word "scarves" written next to it helps the children know where the scarves go at clean-up time and where to find them when they're ready for some creative movement. Don't forget to include task card directions for using the instruments and props in the containers as well. These directions help children understand the proper way to use the materials and enables them to experience success.

Daily Maintenance Checklist

☐ At the end of the day, be sure everything has been returned to its proper place.

☐ Check instruments and props for needed repairs.

☐ Remove any materials that need repairs until they can be fixed.

☐ Tune melody instruments such as autoharps, guitar, or piano as needed.

Teaching Tips

Ask Open-Ended Questions

Visit the music center from time to time to talk with the children about their rhythms, movements, and discoveries. Invite children to teach you rhythms they have created and try to imitate the rhythms yourself by clapping, stamping, or tapping the beat. Use words such as loud, soft, fast, and slow as you describe children's explorations. For example, if one child is playing with cymbals and another is tapping rhythm sticks together, talk about the loud sound made by the cymbals and the soft sound made by the sticks. Refer to Bloom's Taxonomy on page 23 for more questioning ideas.

Try This

"Like" Questions

Ask questions such as:

"Which instrument do you like best?"

"What do you like about it?"

Initiate Creative Movement

You may find, especially in the beginning of the school year, that some materials spend more time sitting on the shelf than they do being used by children. It may be that the children don't know what to do with those materials. Don't hesitate to enter into the music center play. Begin dancing with a scarf or streamer while music is playing. Create free movement by twirling, spinning, and jumping to the mood of the music. Your willingness to respond to music without inhibition will delight the children and will help them begin to set their own creativity free. Invite the children to join you in your dance, and you will soon find a lot of creative movement going on in the music center, with or without your presence.

Offer Guided Practice

There are many excellent movement tapes and CDs on the market that involve listening carefully and following directions. When you introduce a new musical activity such as this, plan to spend some time with the children in the music center helping them listen to the directions and understand how the game works. When you see that everyone knows what to do and the play is progressing nicely, move on to another center and allow the children the freedom, space, and time they need to learn independently. Get the children started in a positive direction, but remember to keep the play child-centered and child-directed.

Tips for Success: Remember to . . .

✮ Show a genuine interest in the children's musical discoveries.

✮ Talk with the children about musical concepts.

✮ Encourage children to use the instruments and equipment properly and carefully.

✮ Make sure that all instruments and equipment have been put away properly at the end of the day.

✮ Check the equipment from time to time to make sure that everything is in good repair.

✮ Check melody instruments once a month for tuning needs.

✮ Remove any broken instruments or equipment.

✮ Help the children get started moving and dancing creatively.

✮ Help children who need technical assistance with CD or tape players.

11

Cooking Center

Through cooking, children can learn about measurement, textures, and tastes. They can learn about different types of foods and can compare foods, noting similarities and differences. Healthy eating habits can be formed by providing frequent activities for learning about and cooking nutritious foods. Children develop self-confidence when they have the opportunity to prepare foods that will be enjoyed by their classmates and teachers. In addition, cooking is a wonderful vehicle for discussing different cultures as well as family traditions. With just a little planning and forethought, cooking activities can be the highlight of the curriculum for both you and the children.

Creating a Cooking Center

There are several areas of the classroom that lend themselves easily to cooking activities. If your class has a daily snack that is

124

prepared and served in the classroom, a special center devoted to cooking is ideal. If a daily snack is not a part of your schedule or if space in your classroom is very limited, cooking activities might be set up in the science center. Either way, the cooking center definitely belongs in the messy area in the wet zone of your classroom.

Essential Materials

If you are planning no-heat activities, setting up the environment for cooking is simple. You will need a clean tabletop, fresh ingredients, measuring and mixing tools, and clean hands. Recipes with pictures are helpful, even for the most basic cooking activities. Children can follow the directions, step by step, and develop their literacy skills along the way.

Placing the cooking table near a water source makes cleanup easier. If you will be using electrical appliances, think about the location of outlets. The table for an electrical appliance should be against a wall with the outlet behind the table so the cord will be out of the way. If this is not possible in your classroom, tape the cord securely to the floor with approved tape to prevent children from tripping as they walk over it. Section off an area of the table with red tape and add a sign that says "Do Not Touch," accompanied by a picture of a hand with a diagonal line drawn across it, to let the children know that the appliance is only for adults to use.

Skillet and Crockpot

Most cooking activities can be done with just two appliances—a deep electric skillet and a crockpot. You can use the skillet for anything that is to be boiled, fried, simmered, or sautéed. With the lid on, the skillet can also serve as an oven for baking. For cupcakes, gingerbread, and all types of batter breads, just pour the batter directly into wax-coated paper cups. Place the paper cups in the skillet, put the lid on, and bake. The bottoms of the cups will darken, but the wax coating prevents them from burning. To bake cookies, line the skillet with a thick layer of aluminum foil. Place cookies on foil, put the lid on the skillet, and bake. For slow-cooking foods such as applesauce, chili, soup, and stew, use a crockpot set on the lowest setting. Make sure that appliances are always attended by an adult or have been placed out of the children's reach.

Keep in Mind

Pay Attention

Never leave the items that are baking unattended.

Slicing Station

You might also set up a slicing station at a cooking table. Young children can begin by slicing soft foods such as bananas, avocados, and cheese with plastic knives. They can also use vegetable peelers successfully with close adult supervision. Show the children how to scrape down and away from themselves and supervise closely. Place paper towels on the table to catch the peelings.

Management Ideas

Handwashing should be the first step in every cooking activity. Be sure to include this step at the top of each recipe card. Always have a covered trash can nearby for all food-related trash. The cover will help keep insects away from your cooking and eating areas and will help you maintain a sanitary environment.

Guidelines for Center Users

When children choose to visit the cooking center, encourage them to:

1. Wash their hands before cooking, eating, or working with food.
2. Keep hands, cooking spoons, and other utensils out of their mouths while cooking.
3. Keep away from areas marked with red tape and "Do Not Touch" signs.
4. Throw away all food-related trash in a covered trash can.
5. Scrape vegetables by pushing the peeler away from themselves while pointing downward.

When you are planning cooking activities, be sure to think the project through from beginning to end, keeping safety constantly in mind. Careful planning and close supervision are critical for the prevention of accidents. Be sure that you have planned for all steps of the activity, including having all of the materials ready when the children arrive, deciding where to put the finished products until it's time to serve them, and letting the children know what to do with dirty dishes.

Teaching Tips

Begin With Simple, No-Heat Cooking Activities

Salads, instant pudding, and sandwiches are fun and easy ways to introduce young children to cooking. They simply require tearing,

Daily Maintenance Checklist

☐ Gather all the ingredients, tools, and equipment for the activity before it begins.

☐ Mark off safety zones with red tape and "Do Not Touch" signs.

☐ Prepare a place to put the finished product until serving time.

☐ Plan for dishwashing using the bucket system if a sink is not available.

☐ Have a covered trash can handy for food scraps.

☐ Provide paper towels or another type of paper covering to catch vegetable peelings if needed.

☐ Wash dishes thoroughly with hot, soapy water or use a dishwasher, if available. Put dishes away in a sanitary storage place.

☐ Make sure all knives have been stored in an adults-only location, out of reach of children.

☐ Remove appliances from center when they are not in use.

☐ Store leftover food items in covered containers.

spreading, or shaking ingredients. For example, tearing several types of lettuce into bite-size pieces and pouring salad dressing over the top makes a super salad that can be prepared independently by most three-year-olds. Making sandwiches with presliced turkey and topping wheat crackers with presliced cheese are just a few examples of simple cooking experiences you can offer with ease in your classroom. When you and the children have had some successful no-heat cooking experiences, you will be ready to move on to more ambitious projects. Careful planning is the key to success.

Try This

Pudding 1–2–3

Instant pudding can be shaken up instead of whipped with an electric mixer.

Encourage Sensory Awareness

Cooking activities, by their very nature, are wonderful opportunities for children to explore all five of their senses. Children can look at the various types of foods and feel the textures in their hands and on their tongues. They can listen to sizzling and popping cooking sounds and smell delicious aromas. And, of course, children will delight in tasting the tempting treats they have prepared. In order to "tune in" to their senses, children need sensitive adults to act as their guides. Ask children questions about their sensory impressions. "What do you hear?" "Take a big breath and tell me about what you smell." "Does that feel like anything else you've ever touched? What?" "What do you notice about the taste?" For more questioning suggestions, see Bloom's Taxonomy on page 23.

Invite Children to Count and Measure

Cooking activities are also custom-made math lessons. Whether the recipes call for a half cup of milk or six eggs, they all include various types of measuring and counting. Invite the children to "read" the recipes themselves and count the number of eggs, discover that one-half cup is less than a whole cup, and so on. This is real-life math, which is so much more meaningful and important to the children than circling objects on a worksheet!

Present Culturally Diverse Experiences

Before bringing a cooking activity into the classroom, get to know your students. Look at the cultural makeup of your class and include foods from each child's native culture. The bounty of delicious foods found all around the world makes it fun and easy to find plenty of recipes that everyone can enjoy. Invite parents or other caregivers to share recipes and lend their assistance in preparing special dishes that are favorites in their homes.

Supervise Activities Closely

Cooking activities must be very closely supervised. It might be wise to recruit an extra adult helper during cooking time. If additional helpers are not available, be sure that the rest of the classroom is low-key and self-managing so that you can devote your attention to the cooking activity. When the activity is finished, be sure to put knives, hot skillets, and other potentially dangerous items safely away and out of the children's reach before you leave the center. While it is important that children not do tasks that can be harmful, doing the entire cooking activity for them while they watch defeats the purpose. Plan carefully, set up a safe environment, teach children how to use appropriate cooking utensils, and invite them to participate fully.

Keep in Mind

Dietary Restrictions

Be aware that some children may have religious beliefs that prohibit them from eating certain foods, and others may have food allergies. If you have students with special food needs and/or limitations, take these into consideration and plan projects in which all the children can participate.

Guide Observations

When interesting and exciting things start happening (such as popcorn kernels popping or scrambled eggs changing states), focus children's attention on the changes. Using open-ended questions, guide their observations so that they observe closely and become aware of the changes that are taking place. Challenge children to recall how the food looked in the beginning of the cooking activity and to describe how it looks now. "Look at the eggs now. Did they look like this when you were stirring them in the bowl? How are they different? What happened? What do you think caused them to change?" For more questioning information, see Bloom's Taxonomy on page 23.

Invite Students to Try New Foods

Some children come to school with very limited taste experiences. They might like macaroni and beans and virtually nothing else.

Cooking activities provide a wonderful opportunity to expand children's tastes and help them discover new foods that they like. Invite and encourage children to taste new foods and provide a good model by always eating some yourself, commenting on how good it tastes. If children say they don't like something based on the way it looks, remind them that their eyes tell them how something looks but only their tongue can tell them how it tastes. Provide encouragement but never force a child to eat anything. If a child comes from a home in which mealtime is a battle of wills, chances are that the child will decline the invitation to try new foods at school. It might take a long time and many cooking projects before that child decides to risk tasting something new, but it will usually happen eventually.

Their Wish, Not Yours

Respect the child's right to choose whether or not to eat something.

Use Nutritious Foods

A lifetime of healthy eating habits can begin in the early childhood classroom. Plan for every cooking activity to involve good, nutritious foods. Talk with the children about the foods that are good for their bodies. During classroom discussions, be careful not to shame or embarrass a child whose family diet may be not as nutritious as it could be. Send recipes and articles on good nutrition home with the children as a model of what is taking place in the classroom. Sometimes a little support from school can make a world of difference in a family's life.

 # Tips for Success: Remember to . . .

- ☆ Talk with children about the sights, textures, smells, sounds, and tastes that they are experiencing.
- ☆ Provide close supervision during all cooking activities.
- ☆ Teach children safe ways to use cooking tools.
- ☆ Make sure everyone has clean hands before cooking or eating.
- ☆ Invite families to share cultural foods and recipes.
- ☆ Eat and enjoy the foods that are cooked in the classroom.
- ☆ Encourage children to try new foods.

☆ Talk casually with the children about good nutrition.

☆ Be sure knives, hot skillets, and other potentially dangerous pieces of equipment are out of children's reach.

☆ Secure electrical cords when you are using appliances.

☆ Read recipes with words and pictures with the children.

☆ Talk with the children about math concepts presented in the recipes.

☆ Avoid using foods that are inappropriate for a child in your group due to allergies or religious beliefs.

12

Woodworking Center

Like cooking, woodworking requires close supervision, and, because of this, it is sometimes overlooked in preschool programs. If adding a woodworking center is something you're considering, here are some benefits. Through woodworking activities, children gain eye-hand coordination, a refinement of small motor skills, and opportunities to invent and imagine. Woodworking also provides opportunities for creative self-expression and growth in self-esteem. Children gain a genuine feeling of satisfaction from actually hammering a nail all the way into a board or sawing a long board in half. With careful planning and preparation, woodworking can be one of the most exciting and valuable centers in your early childhood learning environment.

Creating a Woodworking Center

The key to successful and safe woodworking for young children is *careful planning*. First, think about the location of the center. It needs to be as far away from the blocks center as possible. Wood scraps and wooden blocks may look the same to young children. Avoid the unhappy surprise of finding that your best unit blocks are firmly nailed together by placing the woodworking center on the opposite side of the room from the block center. The center does not require a great deal of space because it will generally be limited to one child at a time. Choose a corner in the classroom, if possible. If space in the classroom is limited, you might prefer to create your woodworking center on the playground. Wherever you decide to place your center, be sure it is in a spot that can be easily supervised at all times. Also, keep in mind that woodworking is noisy, so place the center in your active area where the noise won't be a problem.

Essential Materials

Workbenches

Workbenches are a necessary part of a woodworking center. There are beautiful commercially-made workbenches available in most early childhood equipment catalogs. If your budget won't allow a big expense for woodworking, you can substitute a small, sturdy wooden table and a high-quality C-clamp for a workbench. Be sure to use a table that you don't care about anymore, because it will be full of nail holes and other kinds of damage after just a few days of woodworking!

Safety Goggles

Since safety is an inherent consideration in a woodworking center, provide safety goggles and insist that the children always wear them while engaging in any woodworking activity.

Hammers and Nails

When children are first introduced to woodworking, the only tool they need is a hammer. A lightweight hammer is advisable—one that a young child can lift easily and is small enough to fit in a child's hand. The hammer can simply be stored on the table or in a small box under the table. Introduce hammering to children using a pounding board. This is a wooden board with a number of nails that have already been driven partially into the wood. The child doesn't have to hold the nail steady but just has to make the hammer connect with the nail head a few times.

Another good way to introduce hammering is to use longer nails and empty thread spools. Invite children to place a spool over the place on the board where they would like to hammer a nail. Have children place a nail in the hole in the center of the spool and hold the wide spool instead of the nail while hammering. This reduces the risk of hitting fingers with the hammer but also takes longer for the nail to go all the way into the board. With long nails you also run the risk of a nail protruding through the other side of the board and attaching the board to the workbench itself.

Optional Materials

You might want to introduce a saw, hand-powered drill, screwdrivers, sandpaper, and other tools, one at a time, *after the children have had a lot of experience* working with a hammer and nails. The tools need to be real, not plastic toy tools. Toy workbenches are fine for the dramatic play center, but they don't provide woodworking opportunities. Small woodworking tool kits are available through most school supply houses. Or you can simply visit your local hardware store to find the tools you need.

Keep in Mind

Closet Cleaning

When you clean out closets, keep a woodworking accessories bucket handy. You will be surprised at the things you find that make wonderful additions to the children's projects.

Wood

The best type of wood is a soft pine. Nails go into this type of wood easily. If you have a parent who enjoys building, you should have a rich source of wood scraps in interesting shapes and sizes. You can also visit a lumberyard or a carpentry shop and ask them to save wood scraps for you. You might also visit a high school or middle school to check for discards from wood shop classes. Since large pieces of wood are difficult for small hands to manage, ask your supplier to cut them into manageable sizes for you. A simple box or crate on the floor near the workbench is all you need for wood storage. Check the wood supply from time to time to make sure that you have enough scraps on hand for plenty of creative work.

Odds and Ends

When wood scraps and nails begin to lose their appeal, add new materials to the center. Scraps of construction paper, plastic lids, bottle caps, pieces from discarded cardboard puzzles, and various odds and ends can make interesting additions to construction activities and can revive the children's interest in woodworking.

Provide paint and paintbrushes in the center for children to paint their finished work. Or invite children to take their wood constructions to the art center to add the finishing touches. Be sure to have a place for displaying the finished masterpieces as well. Designate the top of a shelf or a broad window sill in the classroom for displaying these and other three-dimensional works of art.

Management Ideas

Roofing nails are short nails with large, broad heads and work well when young children begin their first attempts at hammering. These nails give the child a bigger target to hit with the hammer, and thus success comes more easily. With just a few strikes a child can drive the nail all the way into a board.

When you have a variety of tools, store them by hanging a pegboard on the wall behind the workbench. Trace outlines of each tool on the pegboard and place the pegboard hooks so that the tools can hang over their outlines.

Guidelines for Center Users

When children choose to visit the woodworking center, encourage them to:

❶ Remember that only one person may work in the center at a time.

❷ Keep all tools and materials within center boundaries.

❸ Keep their eyes and concentration on their work when they are using tools.

❹ Always wear safety goggles.

Daily Maintenance Checklist

☐ Replenish wood and nail supply as needed.

☐ Make sure tools and materials have been returned to their proper places.

☐ Occasionally check tools to make sure that they are in good condition.

☐ Remove anything that needs repair.

Teaching Tips

Set Boundaries and Supervise Closely

With most groups of young children it is a good rule of thumb to make the woodworking center a one-person center. Two or more children wielding hammers while they are close to each other can be dangerous. Closely supervise the woodworker and be sure that the boundaries of the center are clearly defined. If the center is in a corner, use the two walls as two of your boundaries. Create the third and fourth boundaries with colored tape lines on the floor. Allow space for the woodworker to stand and have enough "swing space" for the hammering arm. Make sure that all the children are aware of the boundaries so that everyone's safety is ensured. If you choose to place your woodworking center on the playground, provide the same type of boundary definitions that you would in the classroom. On a grassy area outdoors, the boundaries can be created with tires or crates instead of tape.

Show Genuine Interest in Children's Constructions

The woodworking center is a wonderful place for children to feel competent about their developing skills. You can enhance this feeling by showing genuine interest in the children's constructions, talking with them about their work, and sharing their joy when they accomplish goals. Specific comments about the work itself, such as "You worked for a really long time hammering all these nails into the board," help children develop awareness of the quality of their work.

Encourage Language Development

Language development takes place when you talk with the children about woodworking activities. You can help children develop vocabulary related to size, position, and direction through informal conversations about their work. For example, your comments might focus on size by saying, "I see that you have used two long boards and one short board in your construction." Modeling the use of positional and directional words comes naturally when you talk about the piece of wood on the "top," the "bottom," or in the "middle" and when you notice the nails "beside" the hammer or "next to" the workbench.

Ensure Children's Safety

Help children understand and respect the boundaries of the woodworking center. Make sure that the tools are never taken out of the center. Model ways to hold the tools safely. If your children are very young or inexperienced and are using a pounding board, teach them to hold the hammer with both hands. With more mature children, show them how to hold the nail carefully with their fingers. Keep a constant watch on all woodworking activity in order to prevent nasty accidents.

Encourage Problem Solving

As with all of the other centers in your classroom, woodworking will be successful and positive for the children if you treat their ideas, problems, and efforts with respect. Talk with them, guide them, and provide materials for them, but encourage children to take the time and space to work out their own problems. While it may be difficult to watch them struggle to get a nail to lie flat against a piece of wood, avoid the temptation to jump in and do it yourself. If a child's safety is not a concern, give children freedom to solve their own problems.

 ## Tips for Success: Remember to . . .

⭐ Make sure that children wear safety goggles at all times.

⭐ Reinforce safety rules.

⭐ Show a genuine interest in the children's work.

⭐ Encourage the children's creativity and experimentation.

⭐ Supervise activities closely.

⭐ Check the wood and nail supply periodically and replenish as needed.

⭐ Make sure tools are in good repair.

13

Clay and Dough Center

An area in the classroom, on the playground, or in both places is needed for clay and dough activities. Working with clay and dough is important for the development of the small muscles in a child's hands and fingers and will be especially appealing to the child with a lot of bodily kinesthetic intelligence. Soft, pliable dough is great for pounding out frustrations and angry feelings, so it provides a soothing activity for a child who is upset. Eye-hand coordination and creative self-expression are also developed through clay and dough activities, meeting the needs of the visually-spatially intelligent learner.

Creating a Clay and Dough Center

The clay and dough center can be a separate center located near the art center or it may be a small area located within the art center. If there is simply no space available in the classroom for a clay and dough table, be sure to add clay and dough activities on the art shelf as choices.

Essential Materials

If you have the space and desire to make a separate center, you'll need to provide a child-size table and chairs and a low, open shelf to hold materials. A couple of plastic crates turned on their sides can make nice "shelves" for this area.

Keep in Mind

Dough Duration

Once a batch of dough has been made, it will keep for at least a month if it is stored in a covered container.

How to Make a Batch of Colored Play Dough

2 cups water
2 cups flour
1 cup salt
2 tbsp cooking oil

4 tsp. cream of tartar
paste food coloring or tempera paint

Mix paint or food coloring into two cups of water. Use enough coloring to get a strong, deep color. Remember that the color will be weakened when you add the other ingredients, so make it much darker than you want the finished dough to be. Place flour, salt, and cream of tartar in an electric skillet. Add the colored water and oil. Cook over medium heat, stirring constantly. When the mixture forms a ball, remove it from the skillet and knead until smooth and cool.

Containers

Provide containers of clay or dough on the shelf. Homemade dough is a standard material for this center and should be available all year. There are many simple, easy recipes available. Most doughs are made from everyday pantry supplies like flour, salt, oil, cream of tartar, and water. Making the dough could be one of the class's cooking activities once a month or so. You might also want to add color to your homemade dough to correspond to your projects. For example, fall dough could be orange and brown while white play dough with a little silver glitter paint adds interest to a winter study. To get strong, brilliant colors, use tempera paint or the paste-type food coloring that is used for cake decorating. This type of coloring is more expensive than the liquid you buy in the grocery store, but it is so concentrated that you only need a tiny amount, and a small jar will last for several years. The colors are so strong and true that you can get a true deep red and a very dark black as well as a whole host of interesting shades in between.

Clay and Clay-Like Materials

Potter's Clay

From time to time, offer real potter's clay. This clay comes in either red or gray varieties. And both tend to be very messy. Make your life easier by planning in advance for mess management! You can help make this activity easier to manage by covering the work area with a vinyl table cloth and providing plenty of paper towels and buckets or bowls of water for washing hands before leaving the table. With potter's clay, you'll want to avoid using newspaper. The clay sticks to the paper and makes a bigger mess! Washing clay down the sink can cause plumbing problems, so plan for bucket or bowl washing when you provide this activity. You may want to use potter's clay outdoors because of the mess management problems it can present in the classroom. Potter's clay can be either air-dried or fired in a kiln.

Modeling Clay

For variety, you might occasionally add modeling clay. Plasticine is a type of modeling clay that is available in the toy department of variety stores, or it can be ordered from school supply stores. Plasticine is very hard and difficult to manipulate at first but becomes soft and pliable with work and the warmth of hands. I would advise that you avoid using cookie cutters when working with plasticene clay. The clay sticks to the cutters and is very difficult to remove.

How to Make a Batch Of Gak

Recipe 1

Mix equal parts of glue and liquid starch together in a bowl.

Pour off the excess liquid and you have a batch of gak.

Recipe 2

For a sturdier texture, you can use a slightly more complicated recipe.

2 cups white glue

1 1/2 cups water (room temperature)

2 tsp Borax

1 cup hot water

food coloring or tempera paint

Mix food coloring or tempera paint into 1 1/2 cups room temperature water. Combine the colored water and glue in a small bowl. Pour the hot water into a larger bowl. Add the Borax, stirring until dissolved. Pour the glue mixture into the larger bowl. It will thicken immediately, making stirring difficult. Mix well. Pour off excess liquid. Let the gak "rest" for a few minutes. Pour onto a tray or into a shallow dish. Let it set for about ten minutes and your gak is ready for play. Store the gak in a reclosable container. It should last for several weeks.

Gak

An interesting alternative to clay and dough is "gak." Gak is a stretchy, putty-type dough that will stretch and snap. This material needs no accessories at all. It is fascinating to play with all by itself. There are two basic recipes for gak on the previous page.

Individual Work Areas

To create individual work areas, provide smooth cutting boards, cafeteria trays, or vinyl placemats. For the first few weeks, it is usually best to provide just the dough, without accessories. Encouraging the children to use their hands and fingers to roll, pat, and pinch the dough into shapes helps develop small muscle control and dexterity. After a few weeks, you might add a basket with some accessories like rolling pins, plastic knives, pizza cutters, and cookie cutters. Plastic cookie cutters in interesting shapes can add variety and interest to the center as the year progresses. Collecting plastic cookie cutters in shapes that relate to your projects will help you integrate clay and dough work with the rest of the curriculum. For example, cookie cutters in the shape of various types of leaves could be added when you study the fall season.

Keep in Mind

Avoid Metal Cookie Cutters

Metal cookie cutters are not recommended. They tend to have very sharp cutting edges, and they rust easily because of the high salt content of the dough.

Guidelines for Center Users

When children choose to visit the clay and dough center, encourage them to:

1. Keep the clay or dough on their own board while they are working.
2. Return the clay or dough to its covered container when they are finished.
3. Put all tools away.
4. Keep the dough out of their mouth.

Management Ideas

The clay and dough center is one of the simplest centers in the classroom and it requires very little daily care.

Empty, plastic, ready-to-spread frosting cans make excellent containers to store dough and gak. They are the perfect size to store individual portions.

Daily Maintenance Checklist

☐ Make sure the dough containers are covered tightly at the end of the day.

☐ Check rollers, cookie cutters, and other accessories for cleanliness and needed repairs.

☐ Replace dough as needed.

Teaching Tips

Show Interest and Ask Questions

The clay and dough center is a very child-directed area in the classroom. It does not require a lot of supervision or adult involvement in order for the children to function successfully. However, as with all activities, there are always opportunities in this center to talk with children, show interest in their work, and ask questions that will extend creativity and thinking. For questioning ideas, refer to Bloom's Taxonomy on page 23.

Encourage Experimentation

Ask children questions, such as "I wonder what would happen if . . ." to encourage them to try new ideas. Children can experiment with color combining by mixing two or more primary colors of dough. For example, if you provide red, blue, and yellow dough, ask children what will happen when they mix two or more of the colors together. Add white play dough from time to time so that pastels can be created, and add black dough so children can make darker hues. When you provide white, red, black, and yellow dough, children can experiment with mixing colors to match their skin tones! Encourage the children to guess the outcome of a color-mixing experiment before actually trying it. It is always such a delightful discovery for young children to see purple or green appearing right before their very eyes.

Involve Children in Making Dough

When you see that the dough is getting dry and crumbly, invite the children to help make a new batch. Move into the cooking center and use one of the wonderful recipes available in the resource books. Create a new batch or two of dough to take back to the clay and dough center. As with all cooking activities, prepare the activity and work area by planning for and collecting all materials and ingredients. Make a recipe chart with step-by-step instructions to ensure students' success. Tape off a safety zone if the recipe requires the use of a hot skillet.

Use Dough Play to Release Emotions

Keep in mind that dough can be a soothing activity for children with ruffled feelings. If you see a child is having a difficult day, you might suggest playing with dough for a while. Dough play is also a great alternative to offer children who are taking out their anger in inappropriate ways. You might say to a child, "I see that you are really angry. It is not okay to hit other children, but you can hit the dough as hard as you like. Would you like to try?" This gives the child a safe way to release feelings without exhibiting aggressive behavior toward other children.

Watch for Dough Eaters

If you use homemade dough made from nontoxic ingredients, children will not be in any danger if they taste a bit of the dough.

Most dough recipes call for a lot of salt, and the taste is not one that will encourage eating very much of it. However, if you see a child eating the dough, you might offer a gentle reminder, "Dough is for your hands. Show me what you can make with your dough."

Encourage Creativity and Imagination

Dough sculpting can be a creative art activity for children. Invite children to freely experiment and explore the texture and properties of the dough and to design their own original creations. Scaffold their learning by showing interest in their work while providing them the time, space, and freedom to work independently.

 # Tips for Success: Remember to . . .

- ✰ Make sure that fresh, soft dough is available.
- ✰ Show a genuine interest in the children's work.
- ✰ Understand that it is the *process*—not the product—that is important in children's dough creations.
- ✰ Involve the children in making fresh batches of dough.
- ✰ Vary the type of clay or dough that you offer.
- ✰ Store clay and dough in covered air-tight containers.

14

Construction Center

The construction center is a place for children to build and create with small, open-ended materials. Construction materials are naturally appealing to young children, so children will be drawn to this center without much encouragement or introduction. This is especially true for the children who have a high level of visual-spatial and bodily kinesthetic intelligence. At the same time that they are enjoying using the materials, they will be developing small muscles, eye-hand coordination, oral language, cooperative skills, and creativity. The construction center is one of the most completely child-directed centers in the classroom. The materials are self-explanatory, open-ended, safe, and non-messy so that there is very little need for adult supervision. The center almost runs itself!

Creating a Construction Center

The construction center does not require proximity to water or electrical outlets, so it can be placed most anywhere in the dry region of the classroom.

The construction center is somewhat similar to the blocks center. The materials are used to build and create structures. If space is limited, you can incorporate this center into the blocks center. However, keep in mind that in the blocks center, the main purpose is the way the unit blocks fit together in mathematical proportions. The construction center materials don't fit into that mathematical relationship, and they can be a distraction to the discovery learning that takes place with unit blocks if they are in the same space. Some construction center materials may also be similar to those found in the manipulative center, and some teachers choose to combine the two. The primary difference between construction center materials and manipulative center materials is that most of the manipulative center materials are "closed," having one right way to put the pieces together. Construction materials are "open," in that they present many possible combinations.

Essential Materials

Furniture needs for the construction center are very simple. Provide low, open shelves to hold the equipment. No tables or chairs are required since the type of play that happens here readily lends itself to floor space. It is a good idea to have a low-napped rug covering the floor to make the work area more comfortable for children and to absorb noise. Like all of the other centers, you can use colored tape, walls, and the backs of shelves from other centers to mark off the boundaries of the center.

Basic equipment for the construction center includes interlocking plastic bricks, tabletop blocks, interlocking logs, plastic pipes with connectors, ABC blocks, and numeral blocks. You may be familiar with these items as Legos, Tinker Toys, Lincoln Logs, and so on.

Management Ideas

To prevent confusion at clean-up time, make sure that each type of material has its own labeled storage container. You can place each

Guidelines for Center Users

When children choose to visit the construction center, encourage them to:

❶ Return materials to the proper containers.

❷ Take apart only their own constructions.

❸ Keep the construction center materials in the construction center.

type of material in a resealable clear plastic storage tub or shoe box. The clear plastic helps the children see the materials at a glance. An alternative storage option is a cardboard box that has been covered with self-adhesive paper to make it attractive and durable.

Whether you choose plastic or cardboard boxes, be sure to place a label on the front of the box that has a drawing or a photograph of the contents along with the words to label the container. Matching labels for the shelves provide clearly marked places for everything and also help maintain a sense of order and purpose. It also prevents frustration when a child is looking for a particular type of material and can't find it because it has been jumbled together with other things.

Teaching Tips

Encourage Literacy

If boxes and other containers for materials are labeled with pictures and words, literacy develops as children read the signs to find out where to put the materials away at clean-up time. Keeping a basket of writing materials in the construction center supports children who want to write signs and labels for their constructions.

Talk With Children About Their Work

Although little supervision is needed at this center, your interest in the children's discoveries is always welcome and will enhance learning. Talk with the children about their work. Ask open-ended questions and make comments about specific features of the constructions in progress. Point out the ways constructions are balanced or talk about the colors and numbers of pieces that the children use. If two or more children are using the same type of materials, discuss the ways their creations are alike and different.

Daily Maintenance Checklist

☐ At the end of the day, check to see that all materials have been put away properly.

☐ Sort through the boxes from time to time to make sure that materials have not been mixed. (You might need to do this daily during the first few weeks of school. Later on, a checkup once a week will be enough.)

☐ Be sure materials are in good condition. Remove any pieces that are broken.

☐ Rotate the types of materials every two or three weeks. When you see that the children have tired of a particular type of material, take it out for a while and replace it with something new and interesting.

Honor Children's Accomplishments

Designate a shelf top or window sill in or near the construction center as a display area. Encourage the children to make signs to tell about the constructions and leave them in the display area for a few days to be admired by their peers. If a camera is available, take a picture of the masterpieces so children can have a permanent reminder of their work when its time to return the pieces to the box.

Tips for Success: Remember to . . .

- ✯ Talk with children about their work, and ask open-ended questions.

- ✯ Make specific comments about features of children's work (color, shape, size).

- ✯ Provide a display area for completed constructions.

- ✯ Label boxes and containers with pictures and words to help clean-up time work smoothly.

- ✯ Take pictures of constructions from time to time.

- ✯ Provide task cards when you see that additional challenges are needed in the center.

- ✯ Provide writing materials for children to use to make signs and messages.

- ✯ Check the center from time to time to make sure materials have been returned to their proper place.

15

Sensory Center

Playing with sensory materials such as sand and water is soothing and comforting to young children, especially those with high levels of bodily kinesthetic intelligence. Development of eye-hand coordination and small muscles are encouraged through sensory play. Language skills are enhanced when children talk about their work and the ways the various sensory materials feel and behave. Sensory play is also a wonderful way to teach concepts related to size, measurement, properties of matter, floating and sinking, and other scientific principles. There should always be an area in the classroom, on the playground, or in both places for sensory exploration.

Creating a Sensory Center

The sensory center is a messy center that works best in your wet region where spills are easily managed. Because of the types of activities that are provided in the sensory center, many teachers choose to locate it next to or as a part of the science center. Many scientific concepts are developed through sensory play.

If your whole classroom is carpeted and you don't have a viable wet region, place a sheet of heavy plastic under the sensory table to help protect the floor. Extend the plastic far enough beyond the table so that there is room for the children to stand on the plastic as they stand around the table. Tape the plastic securely to the floor on all four sides so that there will be no loose edges that children could trip over. If this type of space is not available either, then it's a good idea to set up a sensory area outdoors.

Essential Materials

Tables

High-quality commercially made sensory tables are available from school supply stores and catalogs. They are sturdy and will last for many years of sensory play. One especially nice feature of the commercial tables is that most of them come equipped with a drain so you can clean the table without bailing out the water or struggling to carry a heavy container to the sink.

If you don't have access to or funds to purchase a sensory table, you can still create an inexpensive but effective sensory play area in your classroom. One way to solve the problem is to place a plastic baby bathtub on top of an old coffee table. This creates a sensory center that is just the right height for young children. The baby bathtub has a drain so you can easily empty the tub without a lot of lifting and hauling. Another option is to provide individual sensory tubs. These can be created by simply placing dishpans atop a child-size table. Placing a thick, absorbent towel under and around the dishpans will help take care of spills.

Water, Soap, Sand, and More

While water is one of the best sensory materials and should be made available frequently, provide a variety of sensory materials throughout the year. Vary the water play experience by adding food coloring or a few drops of liquid soap. When it seems that the children are ready for a change, take away the water and fill the tub with sand. Other materials you can place in the sensory table or tub include pea gravel, potting soil, perlite, packing foam, shaving cream, aquarium gravel, crushed eggshells, confetti, crushed dry leaves, and sawdust. Some teachers use flour, cornmeal, cornstarch, rice, dried beans, and dried corn as alternative materials in their sensory tables, while others prefer to use only non-food items.

Basters, Egg Beaters, Sifters, and More

To enhance the quality of play at the sensory table, add interesting tools such as plastic tubing, basters, egg beaters, funnels, measuring cups, containers of different sizes and shapes, spoons, scoops, and sifters. When water is used, keep a sponge mop nearby. If you cut the handle down, the mop is child-sized but much more effective than a toy mop. Extra absorbent towels are also good to have on hand in the event of big spills. When a dry material is in the tub, keep whisk brooms, dust pans, and trash cans handy so that spills can be swept up and thrown away easily.

Keep in Mind

Tools Can be Used for Learning—and Cleaning

Remember to provide clean-up tools along with other tools.

Management Ideas

To maintain a healthy environment in your classroom, take the time each day to empty, clean, and disinfect the sensory tub or table. A solution of water and bleach is an inexpensive and effective disinfectant.

You can prevent a minor disaster by locating the sensory center far from the blocks and dramatic play centers. If the sensory table is too close to the blocks center, children are tempted to place the blocks in the water. Blocks are expensive materials, and water-logging them isn't good for their life expectancy. Proximity to the dramatic play center invites children to drip water from the sensory table across the floor to the play sink.

Guidelines for Center Users

When children visit the sensory center, encourage them to:

❶ Wash their hands before and after playing.

❷ Mop and sweep up any spills as soon as they happen.

❸ Keep sensory materials away from their mouths.

Daily Maintenance Checklist

☐ Check to see that the sensory center equipment is in good condition.

☐ Repair or replace materials as needed.

☐ Empty and disinfect sensory table.

Children also tend to place dress-up clothes, dishes, and dolls in the sensory table. While this type of play and combination of materials may be creative, it tends to make classroom management difficult. Wet dress-up clothes and slippery floors can create problems and safety hazards.

Teaching Tips

Encourage Experimentation

Stop by the center from time to time to talk with the children and listen to their comments. Ask open-ended questions while the children make discoveries. Ask questions about which containers children prefer, how many small scoops they predict it will take to fill a container, and what will happen if they whip soapy water with an egg beater. Encourage the children to experiment for themselves and to find their own answers to these and other questions. For more questioning information, see Bloom's Taxonomy on page 23.

Stimulate Sensory Awareness

In addition to questioning and encouraging discoveries, try making specific comments about the materials the children are using. Mention the softness of the shaving cream, the coolness of the water, and the sound gravel makes when it is poured through the funnel. Invite children to describe what they are seeing, feeling, hearing, and touching.

Anticipate Student Needs

Observe play in the sensory center and stay alert to signs that new materials need to be added or that old equipment should be removed for awhile. If children stop choosing the center or if they are misusing materials, this can be an indication that they have lost interest and it's time to change the materials.

Tips for Success: Remember to . . .

- ✿ Talk with the children about their discoveries and experiments.
- ✿ Make specific comments about the equipment and materials.
- ✿ Ask open-ended questions that will stimulate children's thinking.
- ✿ Provide new materials periodically to keep interest level high.
- ✿ Keep a child-size mop, dustpan, and broom handy for cleanup.
- ✿ Stay alert to spills that will create a dangerously slippery floor.
- ✿ Remind the children to wash their hands before and after playing in the center.

16

Outdoor Play Center

Learning happens all day long, whether the children are indoors or out. Therefore, outdoor play is an important part of the total learning experience in an early childhood program and should be built into the daily schedule all year round, weather permitting. The outdoor learning environment is especially important for children who have naturalist and bodily kinesthetic intelligences. Because outdoor play is so valuable to children's well-being, careful preparation is required. With a little planning, your outdoor learning environment will become a natural extension of the classroom.

Creating an Outdoor Play Center

Art activities tend to be especially appealing to children when they are offered outside. Many children who rarely choose the art center in the classroom are drawn to outdoor art activities. You can set up an old picnic table or card table outdoors to create an on-the-spot art center. Children can finger paint, draw with colored chalk, sculpt with potter's clay, and spread shaving cream on the table surface. When the activity is over, clean-up is easy. Just turn the table on its side and hose it off with water.

Essential Materials

Easel

Easels are great additions to the outdoor learning environment. You can set up a regular free-standing easel from the classroom or you might build a special easel mounted to a wall. A simple way to create an outdoor easel is to build a small ledge with holes for paint containers. Attach a lip to the edge and lean a board against the wall. This type of easel is inexpensive and easy to build. Another quick and easy outdoor easel is one made from plastic pipe and attached by S-rings to a chain link fence. You can also make a portable tabletop easel. Take a sheet of sturdy cardboard and cover it with self-adhesive vinyl. Fold the cardboard in half, making a tent-like structure. Attach string from one side to the other to keep the easel from collapsing, tape some large sheets of paper in place and you have an easel ready to go anywhere you like!

"Mural" Materials

You can also set up a mural-style painting experience outdoors by attaching a piece of string from one end of a nearby wooden fence to the other. Use clothespins to attach a long sheet of butcher paper to the string. If you are using a chain link fence, simply attach the clothespins directly to the fence. Provide buckets of tempera paint with large paintbrushes, squirt bottles filled with colored water, or basters with buckets of thin paint. Invite children to paint on the butcher paper. Chain link fences and lines attached to wooden fences also make good drying areas for wet easel paintings.

Sensory Table

A sensory table filled with water makes a great place to cool off on a warm day. Mud play is also an interesting offering for the outdoor sensory table.

Sand Table or Sand Box

Of course, sand is a standard part of most early childhood outdoor environments. Provide a sand table or an elevated sand

box. Add plenty of containers and scoops in all shapes and sizes to make sand play interesting and inviting to children. There is rarely a need to buy sand toys because so many household discards work beautifully. Dampening the sand from time to time enables the children to explore the difference in texture between wet and dry sand.

Woodworking Surface

Woodworking lends itself well to outdoor play. If a woodworking bench isn't available, an old table that is child-height or even a tree stump will do. Add a box of wood scraps, a hammer, nails, and other tools as the children become ready for more sophisticated woodworking experiences. Be sure the woodworking center is in a supervised, out-of-the-way corner so that the carpenters can work safely.

Equipment for Active Play

One of the main purposes of an outdoor area is for children to use their large muscles as they exercise their bodies. Equipment for

active play varies widely from playground to playground. Some basic needs include safe, well-built equipment for swinging, sliding, and climbing. Create a cushioned fall zone under and around all climbing equipment. Create a wheel toy track for tricycles and other wheel toys. Provide hoops, balance beams, balance boards, tunnels, ladders, and tires to make active play varied and challenging for children.

Special Sites

Garden

Gardening is a natural in the outdoor area and can take place year round in warmer climates. Choose a spot for your garden, preferably in a protected area close to a building or a fence. Prevent weeds by lining the area with sheets of heavy plastic. Next, place old tires on the plastic. Fill each tire with a thin layer of rocks and then cover the rocks with soil. Invite the children to plant seeds inside the tire rings, water them, and watch the gardens grow. With careful planning, the children will be able to harvest crops throughout the school year.

Resting Place

A resting place is desirable in the outdoor area for children who are tired and need to cool down or for children who prefer quieter activities. Placing a basket of books and puzzles on a blanket under a tree or in another cozy spot will encourage quiet outdoor moments.

Dramatic Play Area

To support dramatic play outdoors, try mounting a small steering wheel to a saw horse. You might also provide other types of equipment, such as dishes, pots and pans, and a box of dress-up clothes. Keep outdoor dress-up clothes simple so that they do not inhibit children or create safety hazards as they run and climb.

Management Ideas

When you are sharing the playground with other classes, communication among staff members is vitally important. Talk with fellow staff members and reach agreements about the guidelines that will be enforced by all adults on the playground. Explain the guidelines to the children so that safe, happy, and productive play will be possible.

Most of the materials and equipment in the outdoor area will remain in place all the time. Because of the permanent nature of the equipment, setup time is quick and easy.

Guidelines for Center Users

Since each outdoor learning environment is unique, it is not possible to develop a list of limits that will apply to every situation. For example, if a slide is high and narrow or if many children are waiting on the ladder for a turn, climbing up the slide is a potential safety problem. In other settings, on a playground with many slides that are wide and low and that lead to a broad platform at the top, climbing up the slide can be an interesting and challenging opportunity for development. Look at your own setting and decide on guidelines and limits that are necessary in your situation.

Guidelines for Center Users

Consider the following questions.

❶ Will this behavior harm anyone?

❷ Will this behavior infringe on anyone's rights?

❸ Will this behavior damage property?

If the answer to all three questions is "No," then the behavior probably is acceptable and should be permitted. If the answer to any of the questions is "Yes," the behavior needs to be stopped and redirected. Help the children understand why a particular behavior is unacceptable and guide them in finding appropriate ways to meet their needs. For example, if a child is throwing sand, you might explain, "Sand is for digging. Throwing sand hurts people's eyes." If it seems that the child has a need to throw something, you might offer something that is appropriate to throw, such as a soft playground ball.

Daily Maintenance Checklist

☐ Provide paints for the easel and fence art and additional materials for art table activities.

☐ Gather books and puzzles for the outdoor quiet area.

☐ Provide sand toys, wheel toys, dress-up clothes, and other portable equipment.

☐ Check equipment and materials periodically for repair needs.

☐ At the end of the day, make sure that all materials that need to be stored have been put away.

Teaching Tips

Be Alert, Aware, and Involved

If outdoor play is going to be a valuable learning experience, you need to be as involved in children's learning activities outside as you are inside the classroom. Move about the play area and talk with children about their discoveries. Many interesting things can happen outdoors! Be on the lookout for the wonderfully "teachable moments" that nature provides. When you notice an interesting insect, an unusual cloud formation, or leaves beginning to change colors, share your discoveries with the children. Many excellent nature activity books are available that can help you plan for exciting outdoor experiences. Tune in to the beauty and wonder of the natural world and share your joy and enthusiasm with the children. You will find that it is highly contagious.

Supervise Children Closely

Because of the active nature of outdoor play and the larger area to supervise, be especially alert to safety concerns. It is wise for more than one adult to be in the play area at all times. This enables one adult to respond to an accident or emergency if one arises, while the other remains with the group. Dividing the playground into supervision areas makes supervision easier. Position yourself so that you can constantly scan your area of responsibility. Stay alert to potentially dangerous play situations and move close to the children involved to prevent accidents before they happen. Keep an eye out, too, for children who are most likely to tease or bully when not under your direct supervision. Calm and quiet redirection will take care of most problems before they arise.

Tips for Success: Remember to . . .

✫ Provide for outdoor play daily.

✫ Plan for and set up a variety of play experiences in the outdoor area.

✫ Think of the outdoor area as an extension of the classroom.

✫ Talk with children and show interest in their discoveries.

✫ Stay on the lookout for natural wonders to share with the children.

✫ Choose a specific area to supervise and remain in or near that area during outdoor play time.

✫ Work with fellow staff members to define guidelines for playground behavior.

✫ Check equipment and materials periodically for repair needs.

Part III

Just About Everything Else

17

Classroom Management, Schedules, and Routines

After your centers have been created and you have decided how many children each center can accommodate at one time, you need to develop and implement a classroom management system.

Planning Boards

Planning boards are useful classroom management tools. With younger preschool-age children, planning boards are most effective when they are placed in each center. To make signs for individual centers, choose a spot in each center such as a place on the wall or on the back of a shelf. In this spot, make a sign, using pictures or photographs of the center, and words to label the center. Provide a way for children to place name tags on the sign. You might use magnetic strips, book pockets, or plastic hooks. Then make name tags for each child, including the child's photograph and printed name. Laminate the name tags for the sake of durability. Then prepare them for use with the center signs as needed by attaching magnetic strips or punching holes and attaching strings for hanging on hooks.

When it is time for children to select centers, they take their name tags and place them on the center signs. When all of the spaces on a center sign are filled, the center is closed until someone chooses to move to another center. At that time, the child takes his or her name tag from the center sign and moves it to another center. To ensure that there are always plenty of choices, plan for about 2-½ times as many spaces as there are children in the group.

For older four- and five-year-olds, a central planning board works well. A central planning board can be a free-standing board or a centrally located bulletin board. Prepare the board by placing pictures or photographs and written labels for each center, spaced evenly about on the board. Post identical labels on the walls in each center. Under each picture label on the planning board, attach plastic hooks, magnetic strips, or book pockets—one space for each child who can use the center. If you use hooks, hot glue will ensure that they are permanently attached to the board. Then prepare name tags for each child. When children are ready to go to the learning centers, they go to the planning board, choose their centers, and place their name tags in the area indicated for that center on the planning board. The child who chooses to move to another center returns to the planning board and moves the name tag to another center. If there are no empty spaces in a center's area on the planning board, the center is full and the child must make another choice or negotiate with the children in the center for a resolution to the problem. Once established, a classroom management system like this helps your days go smoothly and helps children learn to make choices and work cooperatively with others.

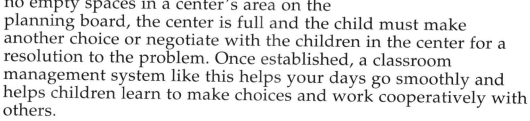

Name Tags

Name tags for the planning board can be simple construction paper shapes that you have laminated, or you can make more durable tags with small wooden hoops that are used for framing tiny needle point decorations. These wooden hoops have a built-in eyelet for hanging. When you first introduce the planning board, it is helpful if each child has a name tag that includes the child's photograph or is unique in some way (color, shape). For example, Roxanne's name tag might be in the shape of a yellow square. She would be the only child in the class whose name tag is that shape and color. The special color and/or shape, along with the child's printed name, helps the children learn to recognize their own names and the names of others.

Task Cards

A high-quality learning environment for young children is filled with such a wide variety and number of choices that there may be literally more than a hundred different activities offered at the same time in one classroom. How can you manage the classroom with so many different choices? One very effective way to put the children in charge of managing their own activities is to provide simple directions with pictures. These directions are commonly called "task cards." Task cards can consist of simple line drawings or stick figures, or photographs of children in the group posted on cards, along with printed words, to give children simple step-by-step directions for activities.

Task cards can be used for daily routine tasks, like handwashing, using tissues, and using the toilet. They can be used for complicated activities such as cooking projects and multi-step science experiences. They are also very useful for daily learning center activities, such as building with blocks and painting at the easel.

Task cards help children understand how to use new and unfamiliar materials. The child can succeed independently without having to wait for an adult to give verbal directions or explanations. Task cards help children develop self-confidence and a sense of security in their ability to manage their own work.

Task cards are also wonderful tools for teaching reading. If reading is defined as understanding the meaning conveyed by written symbols, then reading picture signs and directions is a form of reading that is possible for very young children. This is the beginning of literacy. When you use task cards to explain learning center activities, you are teaching children about reading in a real and meaningful way through all of their daily activities.

Task cards work best when they are very simple. To create task cards for your classroom, begin by thinking about an activity, step-by-step. Then take pictures of a child or children in your classroom to illustrate each step. If, for example, you wanted to serve snacks to your class buffet-style in a special snack center, consider what steps children would need to follow. The first step would be to wash their hands. Take a picture of a child washing hands and add the words, "Wash your hands."

If the snack is served from a basket, photograph a hand reaching into a basket and add the words, "Take a snack." If you want children to sit down while they enjoy their snack, take a third picture showing the same child sitting down and write the words, "Sit at the table." The next picture might show the child eating the snack, and the final step could be a photo of the child throwing away a napkin and a cup.

Digital Photography

Advances in digital photography have made the use of photographs for task cards easy, inexpensive, and accessible to most teachers. There is no need for film and no processing expense. Just plug your reusable chip into the printer and print out as many photos as you want on plain paper! If you don't own a digital camera, put it on your "wish list"—it will make your life as a teacher so much easier! Meanwhile, if photos are not an option for you right now, you can use simple stick figures and line drawings to illustrate your task cards.

Proper Printing

When you make task cards, it is important to write in the manuscript printing style the children will encounter when they enter the primary grades. Always use the standard mixture of capital and lowercase letters when you print. By giving children a good model, you will be getting them off to a solid start for later experiences in reading and writing.

If you make task cards for all types of activities throughout the classroom, you can make your whole classroom self-directed, self-managed, and full of literacy experiences.

Managing Children's Behavior

Children are not born knowing how to get along in society, resolve conflicts, and express their needs in acceptable ways. They need loving, nurturing adults to help them learn these skills. As a teacher of young children, you have the opportunity to help them learn to control their own behavior such that they will become self-controlled, self-directed people who live life with integrity. While this task is no easy job, it is possible with a few guidelines. You can help guide and shape children's behavior in two ways—indirectly and directly.

Indirect Guidance

Indirect guidance is what you do when you prepare the learning environment so that it is responsive to the children's needs. A well-planned classroom provides built-in controls and boundaries. You are indirectly guiding behavior by providing children with a rich variety of choices so that every child will be challenged and involved in purposeful activities. Providing task cards so that children understand how to use materials properly is another form of indirect guidance. Proper scheduling and thoughtful lesson planning will also help prevent many discipline problems from ever occurring. Using planning boards goes a long way to help keep children moving in a positive and purposeful direction.

Direct Guidance

Direct guidance is what you do directly in your interactions with children. It includes intervening and preventing conflicts before they arise, offering alternatives, teaching children about negotiation and conflict resolution, and nurturing children's developing self-esteem.

Offering Choices

One type of direct guidance involves offering choices. For some young children, too many choices can be overwhelming. Inviting a child to do whatever he or she would like to do is too broad a statement and encourages behavior that you might find unacceptable. If you see a child who can't decide what do to, help the process along by narrowing the number of choices to two specific alternatives. For example, "Would you like to build with blocks or paint at the easel?" This type of clearly defined choice respects a child's ability to make a decision while helping the child get started with productive play.

Establishing Rules

Establishing classroom "rules" or guidelines is another form of behavior management. Some teachers choose to establish their guidelines before school starts. The danger in this approach is that the children will then have no say in the process and will feel no ownership for the rules or the classroom. Children may develop an attitude that the guidelines are simply restrictions that make their lives less pleasant rather than understanding why they are necessary.

It is usually much more effective to invite children to create their own "rules" or guidelines. This activity tends to be most effective after a week or two of the beginning of the school year. By that time, there will have been examples of behaviors that have disturbed the peace in the classroom, and you can use them as springboards for conversation. For example, if you see a child hit another child, take some time to talk with them both about the situation. Ask the children what they think about hitting as a means of solving problems and encourage them to discuss alternatives that could be used for handling anger or frustration. When you and the children are ready to write the rules, sit down with a large sheet of chart paper and take dictation, having the children dictate to you the rules that *they* want to establish for the sake of keeping everybody in the classroom safe and happy. Offer guidance to ensure that you end up with a list of rules for the class that are fair, reasonable, and acceptable to everyone. You'll find that children are much more likely to accept and live by rules that they have created themselves rather than rules "imposed" on them by the adults in the classroom.

Try This

Rules on the Wall

When the project is complete, post the rules on the wall at the children's eye level where that they can be referenced as needed.

Negotiating and Resolving Conflicts

Another form of direct guidance involves teaching children how to negotiate with one another and resolve conflicts. Conflicts between children are inevitable. When you see a conflict in the classroom, it's a teachable moment and a time for you to get directly involved. The first step is just to move closer to the children involved. Your physical presence can help them feel safe and secure enough to work on the conflict. They may not need any more help than this!

If children are hurting each other, you need to stop the action immediately. Step in the middle and let them know that you cannot allow people to hurt one another. Next, acknowledge the upset feelings of both parties. You might say something like, "You both look really upset." Helping children identify their feelings can give them the acceptance needed to move on to the next step in problem solving or conflict resolution. If the conflict is about an object, take the object and explain to the children that you are going to keep it while you help them find a way to solve the problem.

Ask the children to tell you about the problem. Get down to their level and listen to each child respectfully. Restate the problem, using positive language. For example, if a child says, "I don't like Summer," restate it as, "You're angry with Summer." Ask the children to propose solutions to the problem. Encourage them to look at each other and listen to each other's point of view. This is very difficult for young children because they are egocentric by nature and have a lot of trouble seeing things from another person's perspective. Don't give up!

Continue restating their ideas and working at helping the children communicate their wants, ideas, and feelings. For example, you might say, "Summer, I hear you saying that you want to play with the truck for five minutes and then give it to T. J. T. J., what do you think about that idea?" Listen to T. J.'s response. If T.J. agrees, move on to the next step, which is providing whatever support the children need in order to put their solution into action.

The final step is to acknowledge the children for solving the problem. If you find that the children are at a stalemate and can't come up with a solution, ask them if they would like to involve another child who might have an idea. You can bring another child into the conversation and ask that child for ways to solve the problem. Another possibility is to ask the children engaged in the conflict if they'd like to hear your idea. If they are in agreement about hearing your idea, you can offer a solution. Whichever route you take, a solution will eventually be found.

The most important thing to remember is to avoid playing the role of problem-solver for the children. The goal is to help children learn ways to negotiate social situations, express their needs and wants, and learn ways to get along in the world with others. If you take over and solve the problems for the children, you defeat the purpose and take away important opportunities for learning.

More Direct Action

There are times, however, when more direct action on your part is required. When someone is injured or something is damaged, you must stop the behavior and let the child know that you are very serious about the fact that you will not allow that behavior to occur. Choose your words carefully so that you are not verbally attacking the child but addressing the behavior itself. While you need to let children know that some behavior is unacceptable, you must be careful to preserve the child's dignity and sense of self-worth. For example, in a situation where a child is hurting another child say, "Hitting hurts. I will not allow hitting in this classroom." Use your words, your tone of voice, your facial expression, and your body language to make it clear that you are very serious.

Keep in Mind

Necessary Intervention

Immediate action is necessary when behavior hurts someone, damages property, or interferes with someone else's rights.

When Unacceptable Behavior Continues

What should you do when unacceptable behavior continues? Imagine a situation in which a child is playing with blocks. The child begins throwing the blocks instead of building with them. This is clearly unacceptable behavior because throwing blocks can hurt someone. First, move into the situation and stop the behavior. Let the child know what behavior is expected. If you have block building task cards, use this as a tool for reminding the child that blocks are for building. A simple verbal statement such as, "Blocks are for building" might also help.

If the child begins throwing blocks again, stop the behavior again and talk with the child about ideas for building with the blocks. Ask open-ended questions to stimulate productive blocks play. Sit down in the center and model appropriate use of the materials. Stay in the center until you feel that the child is engaged in purposeful building and you think the play can continue without your presence.

And what if that willful child begins to throw blocks *yet again?* This time, you need to instruct the child to leave the blocks center. Say something like, "I can see that you are not able to build with blocks right now. I need you to choose another center."

Try This

Follow through, ensuring that the child leaves the blocks center and makes another choice. Some children may resist leaving the center. They may express anger directed toward you, and the words they choose may not be socially acceptable words. Your job is to stay calm, identify the child's feelings, and help the child realize that you accept those feelings by saying, "You're feeling very angry right now. You don't want to leave the blocks center." While you let the child know that you understand and feel empathy, you must also remain firm and ensure that the child does, indeed, leave the blocks center.

Time Out

Removing a child from a center is not the same as giving a "time out." Traditionally, time out involves restricting the child's activity, having them sit quietly in a chair or other designated area of the room for a period of time. Restricting activity is not usually an effective way to deal with the issue and tends to be nonproductive in terms of teaching the child self-control and self-direction. Our goal in managing children's behavior is not to punish and cause suffering. It is about helping children find positive, productive ways to live life in the world with others.

Positive Commentary

When you have removed a child from a center, watch carefully, look for signs of positive behavior and comment on it. If, for example, the child has chosen to throw a ball at a target in the outdoor play area, comment on the careful aim or the strength the child has developed.

Reparation

Another step that sometimes fits into the realm of dealing with unacceptable behavior is asking that the child repair damage that may have been done. If throwing blocks has caused another child's building to be knocked down, the child who threw the block might be asked to help rebuild the other child's building. If a thrown block has caused injury to another child, the thrower might help get first aid for the injured child.

Think about the logical consequences of an action and see to it that they are applied. Again, bear in mind that the purpose is not to punish or to cause pain but to provide the child with a legitimate opportunity to make things right again. Forcing an apology is not a logical consequence and is not appropriate in an early childhood classroom. Teaching a child to automatically say "I'm sorry" is a potentially harmful lesson. If a child who is angry and upset is forced to apologize, the child is learning to be dishonest about his or her emotions. This can cause confusion in learning to deal with powerful emotions, and it teaches that an insincere apology will erase the consequences of an action. A spontaneous, heart-felt apology should certainly be accepted, but the consequence of the actions still need to be handled.

Tantrums

Learning how to manage one's own behavior sometimes involves dealing with strong emotions. At times, emotions may become overwhelming to a child, resulting in an out-of-control tantrum. When this happens, the child needs you to be strong, calm, and reassuring. Recognize that losing self-control is very frightening and upsetting to the child. Stay near the upset child and make sure that the child knows that you are there to keep everyone safe. When the child calms down, offer a friendly hug, a reassuring smile, and an invitation to rejoin the class.

Self-Esteem

Another important aspect of direct guidance is an ongoing effort to build each child's self-esteem. You can accomplish this through activities, songs, stories, and photo albums of the children doing positive things in the classroom. Maintain an overall attitude of acceptance and interest in each child as a unique and special person. If children like themselves and believe that they are capable, competent, likable people, their behavior will reflect that belief and they will be well on their way to self-discipline.

Dr. Dorothea Huddleston, a very wise friend and former professor at Texas State University in San Marcos, Texas, once advised me to "Be firm, be fair, and be friendly, and above all, never wound the heart." If you keep those words in mind as you go about the task of guiding children's behavior, you can't go wrong!

Schedules and Routines

Young children need the security of knowing what comes next and the comfort of following a predictable routine day after day. Develop a daily schedule and adhere to it. Sticking to the exact time on the clock is not a major concern, but following a pattern of activity is important for the children's sense of well-being. A good schedule is flexible but consistent. One way to help children become comfortable with the schedule is to post it in blocks on the wall at the children's eye level, using photographs of the actual children in the class. The blocks might look like this:

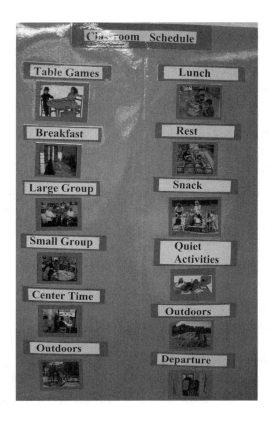

There is no single "right" schedule. Schedules vary from program to program and from classroom to classroom. Some schools have special classes, such as music or movement classes, that are worked into the schedule. Meals are provided in some settings, while snacks are served in others. Some programs are full-day and others are half-day. Whatever your situation, however, there are some basic points to consider when planning your schedule. Provide a balance between active and quiet time; small group, whole group, and individual activities; and child-initiated and teacher-initiated activity. Also plan for and allow enough transition time between activities.

Following are some ideas for daily routine management that will make your day run smoothly and help make even the most ordinary part of the day an opportunity teaching and learning.

Arrival Time

Some children come to school on buses while others arrive in cars or are walked to school accompanied by family members. In some situations, all of the children arrive at the same time. In other programs, children may arrive over a period of 10 or 15 minutes. Whatever the mode of arrival is at your school, it is always important for an adult staff member to be available and ready to greet children at the door. Ideally, this will be the same person every day. A familiar friendly face can erase the stress that some young children feel when they must say goodbye to their families at the beginning of the day.

Staff members who share responsibilities during arrival time must plan together for this important time of the day. Those who are responsible for receiving children must be in place and ready to say "good morning" a few minutes prior to the expected arrival of the first child. Greeting the child by name with a warm and friendly smile can go a long way toward getting the day off to a wonderful start.

In some programs, the children come directly to their classrooms upon arrival. If that is the case in your situation, be sure that the room is ready for action before arrival time begins. In other settings, the children go directly to a cafeteria for a meal or they gather in the outdoor play area. Staff members must be in place and ready to receive children in whichever arrival area is used. The school day begins when the first child comes through the door, so all preparations must be complete prior to that child's arrival.

Materials

Name Tags or ID Bracelets

During the first few weeks of school, it is helpful if the children wear name tags or identification bracelets. The name tags or bracelets should have the child's name and the teacher's name clearly marked. If your program uses buses, the bus number should be included. If name tags or bracelets are used, anyone who sees a child will be able to determine where the child belongs.

Personal Belongings Box

Provide a large box for each group's lunch boxes, backpacks, and other "treasures" if children from several classes gather in a central location like a cafeteria or on the playground. When everyone has arrived, take the box into the classroom so that personal belongings can be put in place for the day. This avoids unnecessary waiting and confusion when it is time for the children to go to their classrooms. This box can also serve as a "Take Home Treasure Box" for personal items such as toys, candy, or money that need to be kept out of children's reach and protected throughout the day.

Circle Time

Circle time can be a very important part of your day—or it can be dreary and difficult to manage. It all depends upon what you do and how you do it! Some younger or less mature preschool-age children are not yet ready for whole group activities. If you insist that they join circle time, they are likely to disrupt the activities you have planned and diminish the quality of circle time for the whole class. Providing an alternative to circle time for those children is in everyone's best interest. Perhaps the child can look at a book or work with dough or clay in another part of the room. If circle time in your classroom is something that is active, engaging, and enjoyable for the other children, the not-yet-ready child will eventually join in.

Keep It Short

Circle times work best when they are brief—no more than 10 to 15 minutes at a time. You might schedule several circle times throughout the day, interspersed among small group and individual activities. Some teachers begin the day with a planning circle, have a music and movement circle mid-morning, a story circle before or after lunch, and a closing circle at the end of the day. These are all appropriate whole group activities that work well for most preschool classrooms.

Keep Children Moving

Circle times also work best when they offer plenty of opportunity for action and involvement. If you include songs, fingerplays, and hands-on opportunities in every circle time, you are likely to have children who look forward to circle time with eager anticipation.

Planning Circle

The planning circle is the time for you and the children to greet one another, find out what's new in the classroom, share news from home, and make plans for the day ahead. Younger preschool-age children plan verbally, telling you and others what they intend to do that day and going to work in the learning centers. Four- and five-year-olds can write their plans every day. Provide planning books for each child by folding sheets of plain paper in half, covering them with a construction paper or wallpaper cover and stapling them in the middle. Label each book with the child's name, post dates on each page, and draw a line across each page dividing it into top and bottom halves. Make sure that you have the correct number of pages for each month. Children use their emergent writing skills to represent their plans for the day in the top section of the page, and "read" their plans to an adult or a friend, place the books in a special basket or box where they are stored, and go to the centers they have selected.

Try This

Routines

You and your students can go through many routines during planning circle time, such as updating the calendar and the weather chart, reading the helper chart, and writing the daily news on the large chart tablet.

Closing Circle

At the end of the day, your older children revisit their planning books as they recall the events of the day and write about them on the bottom of the day's page. Remember that their writing may be pictures, random scribbles, letters, copied words, letters that represent initial sounds, or words written with "invented" spelling. Each child will approach this task at an individual level. Children then may share what they have written with you or a

Try This

Let Parents Know

When the experience chart (summary of the day) is finished, post it by the door so that parents can see what their children have been up to that day!

friend. For younger preschool-age children, the closing circle can be a brief conversation in which children tell about their day. Then the group can contribute to an experience chart in which you write their summary of the day's events. At the beginning of the school year or with a younger group, this may be one brief sentence, such as "We made soup." Later in the year you may fill the page with the children's ideas. If you save each day's chart, transcribe the dictation onto book-size paper and invite children to illustrate the pages; you can create a child-dictated journal that chronicles the entire school year. What a great way to document your year—and to add a meaningful literacy experience to every day!

Meals and Snacks

Mealtime and snack time should be pleasant social experiences for children. It is important for teachers to sit with children and talk with them while they eat. Joining in the meal or snack gives

Keep in Mind

Mealtime Opportunities

Mealtime is a great time to encourage *cooperation* and *responsibility* among children.

you an opportunity to model appropriate table manners and mealtime behavior. Using a helper chart, designate a child who will be the "table setter" for the day. The table setter can pass out cups, napkins, and utensils for each person at the table. Not only does this teach children positive social skills, it's also a great lesson in applied mathematics: one-to-one correspondence. In the interest of developing good eating habits, respect the children's choices about the amounts and types of food they will eat. Encourage them to follow their own appetites and eat as much or as little as they desire. A "clean-your-plate" rule teaches children that they can't trust what their bodies are telling them. Work with the menu planners and meal providers in your program to make sure that every meal is nutritious and then encourage children to choose which foods they will eat. There's never a place for empty calories in a child's diet, and the adults who prepare the foods are responsible for providing a healthful variety of choices.

Self-Help Skills

Eating time is also a time for children to learn self-help skills. Keep a damp sponge, paper towels, and a child-size mop handy so children can clean up their own spills. Help them learn how to open their own milk cartons and cut their own food instead of doing it for them. Too much help or help given too soon interferes with a child's developing sense of independence. Stand back and wait until help is really needed. Even then, provide the scaffolding needed to get the task underway, and then support the child in seeing the task through to completion. Make sure children clean up their own eating area and throw away their own trash.

Alternative Activities During Mealtime

Children eat at different rates of speed. Some linger over a meal while others gobble everything down and are ready for action within a few minutes. Plan for these differences. Provide alternative activities for children who are finished eating. Sitting quietly or waiting are not natural activities for young children. A lot of difficulties can be prevented by planning interesting things to do all throughout the day, including during routine time. Some alternatives at the end of breakfast time include going to the playground, going into the classroom to begin learning center activities, or joining a group of early finishers for songs, stories, and games. If your children eat lunch at school and then stay for naptime, a transition to nap time could include brushing teeth, choosing books to look at independently, removing shoes, and settling down for naps on cots or mats.

Toileting

In an ideal setting, a bathroom is located within each classroom and children are free to use the toilet whenever necessary. Waiting to use the toilet is very difficult for young children and can lead to soiled or wet pants and upset feelings. As much as possible, toileting times need to be dictated by each individual child's needs.

Unfortunately, some buildings do not lend themselves readily to this type of "natural" toileting schedule. If the bathroom is far away from the classroom, make plans to help meet the children's toileting needs. Encourage children to stop by the bathroom when the class is moving from place to place within the building. One adult can stay in the bathroom area while the other adult moves along with the class. At other times, an adult will need to be available to accompany children to the bathroom whenever the need arises. It may be wise to take several children at one time so that the entire day won't be devoted to toileting.

Even in the best-planned facility, toilet accidents will occasionally happen. An extra set of clothes, including socks and underwear, are a must for each child. Ask parents to send a change of clothes on the first day of school. Mark each item with the child's name. Store each child's clothing items in a large, plastic self-closing bag. Mark the

Keep in Mind

Extra Clothes

Some children will come to school without extra clothes. Plan for this by having a few extras on hand.

outside of the bag with the child's name. Store all the bags in a special box so that changes of clothing can be located quickly and easily. When the weather changes, send the bags home and ask for replacements that are appropriate for the season.

Transitions

The bumpiest parts of the early childhood day are transition times. These are the times when you are changing from one type of activity to another. For example, a transition time is when learning center time is over, clean-up time is beginning, and the children are going to gather on the rug for a story after they finish cleaning up. Some children will finish their clean-up tasks before others. If there's nothing for them to do, behavior problems are invited.

Transitions During Class

Think through your day, look for the bumpy times, and plan transition activities to make things run smoothly. One of the most effective ways to handle transitions (that includes changing from an individual activity to a group activity) is for one adult to go to the group time area as soon as a few children have gathered there. This adult starts singing songs or doing fingerplays with the children while the other adult helps the rest of the class finish their clean-up tasks. As children finish cleaning up, they join the group until everyone is together again. Another effective method is to provide a special box or basket of books which is used only for transition times. Children who finish their tasks choose a book to read while they wait for the others to join them.

Transitions Through Halls

Moving from place to place within the school is another type of transition that can be difficult. If you expect children to move through the halls in quiet, straight lines, you could be asking for trouble. It is not natural for young children to walk in silent, single-file lines. The goal is that children can move from place to place in a safe and socially acceptable way. Plan ways to do this that are in keeping with the children's nature. Singing songs that include hand motions, and playing follow-the-leader-type games are some

Try This

Fun Transitions

Invite the children to move as robots, animals, spaceships, and so on. Use your imagination and encourage the children to contribute ideas to help make transitions fun.

ways to move a group of children successfully. Creative movement is another effective method.

Dismissal

Another tricky time of the day that requires careful planning is dismissal at the end of the day. This can be especially difficult if you have several groups of children from different classes who will travel on different buses or in various carpool groups that all leave at the same time.

One way to ease the confusion that can happen at this time is to designate areas for each bus or carpool group in the hallways. For example, the children who ride on bus number 3 can be the "Purple Pig" bus group. Mount a cut-out figure of a purple pig on the wall at the children's eye level in the place where the group is to gather. Post a list of names of children in the group on the wall so the adults can double check to ensure each child is in the correct spot. Give each child in the "Purple Pig" group a big purple ticket when he or she leaves the classroom. Laminate construction paper strips to make tickets. The child matches the color of the ticket with the purple pig. An adult who is assigned to the "Purple Pig" group goes to that area to greet the bus riders and check tickets to make sure that each child is in the proper place. Each group has its own designated area and color, along with an assigned staff member who meets with that group every day.

Waiting Time

Waiting time may be inevitable because of late-arriving buses. Have the children sit down on the floor in their gathering places and sing songs or talk about the events of the day. When it is time for the group to leave, walk them to the bus or car, collect their tickets, and see them off. Return the tickets to the classroom to be used the next day. After the first month or so, most of the children will know their areas and the adults will know their groups, so the tickets will no longer be necessary. It's wise, however, to keep the list of names on the wall throughout the year as a way of checking to see that everyone is together before leaving the building.

18

Special Events

An important part of the early childhood curriculum is to expand children's awareness of the world around them by providing first-hand experiences with real objects, events, and people. These kinds of experiences require that you leave the regular classroom "routines" behind and do something special. You might have a visitor who comes to the classroom to introduce the children to a new idea or you might take the children out into the community. Either way, the success of your venture will depend upon careful planning.

Visitors

Sometimes, the best way to provide a new experience is by inviting someone special to visit your classroom or school. For example, it might not be especially interesting for the children to visit a police station, but a visit from a uniformed police officer could be the highlight of the year. I once had a child whose father was a motorcycle police officer. I spoke with him, got permission from the school administration, and arranged for him to ride his motorcycle with lights flashing all the way through the central hallway of our school. Everyone was amazed to see such a sight, and it marked the beginning of a very interesting project!

If you plan to invite a visitor to your classroom, here are some basic questions to ask yourself.

Are the Children Ready for the Experience?

If you have very young or inexperienced children, new and strange experiences can be stressful and frightening. Before you invite a guest, find out if any of your children are especially upset by loud noises, face masks, animals, or other possibilities. If you have a number of children who are likely to be upset, you might decide to ask the visitor to modify the planned presentation, or you may choose to postpone the visit until a little later in the year when the children have had more time to gain self-confidence and trust.

Is the Visit Meaningful?

Guests in the classroom are most effective when their topic is relevant to the project at hand. For example, if your class is exploring the idea of things that make noises, that would be a great time to invite Samantha's father to come in and play his saxophone. It would be best to reserve the visit from the dentist for another time.

Is the Visitor's Presentation Developmentally Appropriate?

Talk with prospective visitors in advance and explain the developmental levels of the children in your group. Oftentimes, professionals from fields outside of education are accustomed to speaking with groups of older children. They may have preplanned presentations that are too long, too scary, or at a level that is too advanced for preschool-age children to enjoy. Make sure that your guests are ready to use clear, simple language, to provide lots of opportunity for hands-on exploration and action, and to keep their presentations brief. You might also suggest that they introduce loud and potentially frightening things gradually. For example, suggest to the firefighters that they announce that they are going to turn on the fire engine siren and that it will be very loud, rather than having them arrive on the playground with sirens blaring.

How Should You Prepare the Children for the Visitor?

Talk about the visitor and the children's expectations before a guest arrives, just as you do before embarking on a field trip. Write down their questions and predictions and explain your expectations of them. After the visit, talk with the children about the experience and engage them in dictating and decorating an experience chart to post on the wall and to use later as an addition to your class journal. Also be sure to have the children dictate and decorate a "Thank You" note to the visitor, letting your guest know that you and the children appreciate his or her gift of time.

Field Trips

If you decide to take a field trip to enrich the children's learning, the same questions apply that help you determine whether or not to bring in a visitor. In fact, there are even more questions you can ask yourself.

Are the Children Ready to Leave School?

Leaving home and going to school is a big step for many young children. For children who have had little experience away from home, leaving school for a field trip can be frightening. If this is the case with your class, go slowly as you introduce the idea of a field trip. The first couple of months of the school year are probably best spent at school. When the children are comfortable with the school environment, a first field trip might be a leisurely ten-minute walk around the neighborhood. Gradually expand your field trips in terms of distance and time as the children mature.

Is This Trip Meaningful?

Why are you going on this trip? What is the purpose? How does it relate to the current project theme? What will the children gain from the experience? If your class is studying farm animals and you want to expose the children to live farm animals, then a trip to a farm would be meaningful and relevant to the topic.

Is This Trip Developmentally Appropriate?

When you have decided that the trip is meaningful and that it serves a legitimate purpose, the next step is to ask yourself if it is an appropriate experience for *young* children. Many businesses take groups of school-age children on interesting and educational tours of their facilities, but some of these field trips are not appropriate for younger children. The subject matter may not be of interest to young children or the facility may not meet the needs of young children.

For example, a tour of a commercial bread bakery is an excellent experience in social studies for older children. The same bakery tour, however, may be little more than a diversion for young children. Commercial bakeries tend to be noisy places filled with heavy machinery. The traditional tour may take over an hour. The ovens are very hot and are potentially dangerous for active young children, and everything is usually up too high for little children to see. A far better experience for young children is to actually bake bread at school or in a family kitchen or to visit a small neighborhood bakery.

What Do You Know About the Site?

If you hear about a great place you think your class may benefit from visiting but you've never been there, stop by and visit for yourself before you decide to schedule a field trip. Look at the site, ask questions about the tour, and think about how your students will respond to the experience. If you decide that it is a good place to visit, spend some time talking with the potential tour guides about your children's needs. This is the time to consider some practical concerns as well, such as locating the bathrooms and water fountains. If your field trip will be longer than a few hours, make plans for the children to have a snack or a meal. Find out where the children can wash up, sit down to eat, and throw away trash.

Who Will Be Available to Go Along and Help?

Parents are the most common source of help for field trips. In some situations, however, it is difficult for parents to take time away from their work schedules. If this is the case, have their parents check with grandparents or other family members. Sometimes, high school students or college students who are studying child development may be able to assist. Also check with your local churches and service organizations for field trip volunteers. You may be surprised to find that there are many caring people in the community who are eager to help make the world a better place for young children!

The number of adults you will need varies according to the type of field trip you are taking. If you are going to a concert in an auditorium where the children will be seated most of the time, you can probably manage with just a few extra adults. If you are going to a large, open area such as a park, zoo, or a botanical garden, an ideal ratio is one adult for every two children. This gives each child a hand to hold, plenty of individual attention for questions, and the freedom for each small group to venture off to see the things that interest them without having to wait for the whole class.

Are Volunteers Aware of the Goals of the Trip?

Decide what you want the children to learn from the field trip and spend some planning time with your volunteer helpers so that they can be effective facilitators. Share with them your goals for the children and give them some background information so they will be prepared for the trip. It is often helpful to give volunteers an information sheet with facts about the site and ideas for topics to discuss with the children in their group. If you are going to a large place, such as a zoo or livestock show, provide a map that shows the locations of bathrooms, water fountains, and meeting places. Talk with volunteers about the schedule, meeting times, meeting places, and guidelines about buying souvenirs and snacks for the children in their group.

How Will You Get There?

Most programs have buses or vans available for field trips. In some settings, private cars may be your method of transportation. If your program requires that children be transported in private cars, be sure that each child has a seatbelt, each car has two adults so that the driver won't be distracted by the children's needs, and check with your program's regulatory agency and insurance agency to make sure that there are no liability issues. You may also need to check with law enforcement agencies regarding the need for car seats for smaller children.

Do You Have Parental Permission?

It is absolutely *essential* to get written consent from each child's family before leaving for a field trip. You may want to ask parents to sign a generic field trip form at the beginning of the year to cover *all* upcoming trips at one time. Keep these forms in a special field trip file box or folder and *take them with you* whenever you leave the school grounds for a field trip. The form should include the following information.

- Permission to take the child on trips away from the school grounds at the teacher's discretion.
- A statement that the school and the teacher will not be held liable for accidents that may occur while away from school.
- Emergency telephone numbers, including the child's doctor's office.
- Permission to obtain emergency medical treatment for the child if necessary.

Even though the permission form takes the place of having to ask parents to sign releases every time you go somewhere, it is still necessary to let families know about your plans. Send notes home and post a notice in your classroom for several days in advance of the trip. Include information to parents about special items the children will need for the trip, such as comfortable walking shoes or the need to bring a sack lunch.

Is There a Cost for the Field Trip?

Field trips to some places will require an admission fee. Whether the fees are paid by the school or by the parents, be sure to collect the money the day *before* the trip, count it, and have it ready in an envelope (or in the form of a check) so that you won't waste time at the door counting nickels and dimes, or that a child is not allowed to participate at the last minute.

How Should You Prepare the Children for the Field Trip?

Learn Children's Expectations

Before going on a field trip, talk with the children about their ideas and expectations. Find out what they think they might see and what might happen at the field trip site. Turn this into a literacy experience by writing down the children's predictions in the form of a checklist. As you make the checklist, you will become aware of the children's level of knowledge, special interests, and concerns. With this added insight, plan ways to meet the children's needs both during the field trip and as a follow-up experience in the classroom. Take the checklist with you on the field trip.

Share Your Expectations

Talk with the children about your expectations of them. Discuss ways to make the trip safe for everyone, such as wearing seatbelts, staying with adults, and any other safety concerns that you may have about a specific field trip.

Inform Children of the Day's Schedule

Tell the children about scheduling plans, such as whether they will eat a snack or meal at the site and when the class will return to school. Young children have difficulty with time concepts but they can relate to events in their daily schedule. For example, rather than telling children that they will be back at school by 10:30 A.M., they will more clearly understand if you say that they will be back in time for music.

With a little thought, planning, and preparation, field trips and classroom visitors can be wonderful learning experiences that will provide years of fond memories.

19

Parent and Family Involvement

It has been said that parents or other caregivers are a child's first teachers. I believe this is very true. I also believe that they are the child's most influential teachers, especially in the preschool and kindergarten years. Therefore, a very important part of teaching young children is providing resources, information, and support for the families of the children we teach.

This may be easier said than done! Your children might ride buses, carpool, or participate in before-and-after-school child care programs such that you have few opportunities to see their parents[1]. Even when parents transport their children to and from school, arrival and departure times may be too hurried for you to have opportunities for meaningful conversations with them. So what can you do? Here are a few ideas that can help you reach out to parents so that they feel supported and valued by your program.

Personal Phone Calls

Take a few minutes in the evening once a week and telephone one or two of your children's parents. Parents are often surprised to receive a phone call from a teacher, and sometimes they expect that the teacher is calling to report a problem. What a delight it is for them to find out that you just want to get to know them and to let them know how much you enjoy having their child in your classroom!

You can use these informal conversations to share information about upcoming events, to ask for the parents' ideas for a curriculum project you are planning, or to find out if they have any questions or concerns about their child's progress and development. Phone calls are an easy way to build relationships with parents on a casual, informal basis.

To make sure that you have called everyone, keep a list by your phone and check off names as you speak with family members.

Send "Happy Notes" Home

Write "happy notes" to send home with one or two of your children each week. A "happy note" reports good news, such as a book that the child especially enjoyed, a science project that the child found particularly interesting, or a skill the child has recently acquired. The purpose of a "happy note" is to establish a positive relationship with the family, not to give an in-depth progress report. Keep it light and friendly, and, as with the phone calls, keep a list handy so that you can make sure that every child gets to take home happy notes on a regular basis.

---

[1]Although the word "parent" is used here, I recognize that children's caregivers may include aunts and uncles, grandparents, cousins, family friends, or others. Every time the word "parent" occurs in this chapter, it is used broadly to refer to the variety of caregivers who are looking after our children.

Newsletters

Most parents are interested in what their children are doing in school. If you involve the children in creating monthly newsletters to take home, you not only provide information for the parents, you also provide a monthly literacy experience for the children. Some items you might include are scanned copies of the children's artwork, photos of classroom activities, and stories that the children have dictated. You can also use the newsletter to pass along parenting tips, information about child development, or requests for volunteers to help with classroom activities, projects, special events, or field trips. Newsletters that are not too lengthy, are written in a casual, friendly tone, and contain work or photos of the children generally are read and appreciated by parents.

Beautiful Junk

Parents can be a wonderful source of useful classroom items, such as dress-up clothes, dishes, empty food boxes, paper towel tubes, egg cartons, and more. Send home a list of "beautiful junk" that you would like to have donated to your classroom and ask parents to post the list on their refrigerator door at home. You might be amazed at the wonders that will appear! Some teachers keep a box near the classroom door where beautiful junk donations can be deposited. Just be sure to go through it every day and make sure that the items get put away in their appropriate places for later use.

Classroom Visitors

While it is difficult for some parents to find time during the day to visit in the classroom, it is important to let them know that they are always welcome and that their assistance is always appreciated. You might send home a survey at the beginning of the school year asking parents about hobbies, special talents, or skills that they might be willing to share with the children. File these survey sheets away and use them for planning projects. If, for example, Priscilla's grandmother likes to garden, you might ask her to come in and help the class plant a fall vegetable garden as part of a project on plants. Likewise, if you learn that Angel's stepfather is a plumber, you might want to invite him to come for a visit and demonstrate the use of his tools when the class begins a project on "water."

Some family members might be willing and able to help out in the classroom but feel unsure about their roles and responsibilities. It is usually helpful for you to give them a specific assignment, such as reading to small, informal groups in the library center or supervising a cooking project.

Field Trips

You might have a family who raises parakeets at home or a parent who works in the neighborhood grocery store. Taking the class to visit these families at home or at work can be delightful experiences for everyone. Talk with your families and find out what might be possible.

Parents can also make wonderful teaching assistants when the class ventures out for ambitious field trips to the zoo or the park. Always ask for parent volunteers to help with excursions like this. You can use the extra hands, and the parents and children will benefit from having the experience together.

At-Home Projects

You may have parents who would love to help the class but can't get away during the day. Projects like making folder games, planning books, or other "teacher-made" items might be just right for them. You might write a note in one of your newsletters recruiting that kind of help. It can make your life much easier and can provide the parents a way to feel more involved in their child's program.

Whatever level of involvement is possible, remember that you can make a tremendous difference in the life of a family by being available and supportive of them as they go about the enormous task of bringing up children!

Resources

Internet Resources

The following websites offer a wide range of ideas, information, and inspiration for the teacher of young children. Many of them provide links to other helpful websites and opportunities for you to purchase books and videos, join professional organizations, subscribe to in-print or online journals, and to chat with other early childhood professionals.

www.123child.com

www.alltheDAZE.com

www.CommunityPlaythings.com

www.earlychildhood.com

www.kconnect.com

www.ira.org

www.naeyc.org

www.nctm.org

www.princetonol.com

www.seca.org

www.sharonmacdonald.com

www.teachers.net

Books and Articles

A list of quality books and articles on early childhood education could fill an entire book in and of itself! With all due respect to the many wonderful early childhood education authors, I've selected a short list of books and articles that are most relevant to the work we do.

Bloom, B. S. (1969). *Taxonomy of educational objectives: The classification of educational goals*, United Kingdom: Longman Group.

Bredekamp, S., & Copple, C. (Eds.). (1997). *Developmentally appropriate practice in early childhood program (Rev. ed.).* Washington, DC: National Association for the Education of Young Children.

Burns, M. S., Snow, C., & Griffin, P. (1998). *Preventing reading difficulties in young children.* Washington, DC: National Academy Press.

Chard, S. (1998). *The project approach: Making curriculum come alive.* New York: Scholastic.

Cherry, C. (1999). *Creative art for the developing child: A teacher's handbook for early childhood education* (3rd edition). Revised by Dianne Miller Nielsen. Grand Rapids, MI: McGraw-Hill Children's Publishing.

Cherry, C. (2001). *Creative movement for the developing child: An early childhood handbook for non-musicians* (3rd edition). Revised by Dianne Miller Nielsen. Grand Rapids, MI: McGraw-Hill Children's Publishing.

Cherry, C. (2001). *Please, don't sit on the kids: Alternatives to punitive discipline* (2nd edition). Revised by Dianne Miller Nielsen. Grand Rapids, MI: McGraw-Hill Children's Publishing.

Clements, D., & Sarama, J. (Eds.). (2004). *Engaging young children in mathematics.* Mahwah, NJ: Lawrence Erlbaum.

Copley, J. (Ed). (1999). *Mathematics in the early years.* Washington, DC: National Association for the Education of Young Children and National Council of Teachers of Mathematics.

Copple, C., Bredekamp, S., & Neuman, S. B. (2000). *Learning to read and write: Developmentally appropriate practices for young children.* Washington, DC: National Association for the Education of Young Children.

Curtis, D., & Carter, M. (2003). *Designs for living and learning: Transforming early childhood environments.* St. Paul, MN: Redleaf Press.

Feldman, J. (2000). *Transition tips and tricks for teachers: Attention-grabbing, creative activities that are sure to become classroom favorites!* Beltsville, MD: Gryphon House.

Hayes, K., & Creange, R. (2001). *Classroom routines that really work for preK and kindergarten: A Bank Street teacher resource.* New York: Scholastic Professional Books.

Helm, J., Beneke, S., & Steinheimer, K. (1998). *Windows on learning: Documenting young children's work.* New York: Teacher's College Press.

Hirsch, E. S. (1996). *The block book.* (3rd ed.) Washington, DC: National Association for the Education of Young Children.

Houle, G. B. (1984). *Learning centers for young children.* West Greenwich, RI: Consortium Publishing.

Kaltman, G. S. (2006). *Help! For teachers of young children: 88 tips to develop children's social skills and create positive teacher-family relationships.* Thousand Oaks, CA: Corwin Press.

Kaltman, G. S. (2006). *More Help! For teachers of young children: 99 tips to promote intellectual development and creativity.* Thousand Oaks, CA: Corwin Press.

Katz, L., & Chard, S. (2000). *Engaging children's minds: The project approach* (2nd ed.). Westport, CT: Greenwood Publishing.

Kohl, M. F. (1994). *Preschool art: It's the process, not the product.* Beltsville, MD: Gryphon House.

MacDonald, S. (2004). *Sanity savers for early childhood teachers: 200 quick fixes for everything from big messes to small budgets.* Beltsville, MD: Gryphon House.

MacDonald, S. (1998). *Everyday discoveries: Amazingly easy science and math using stuff you already have.* Beltsville, MD: Gryphon House.

McCarrier, A., Fountas, I., & Pinnel, G. (1999). *Interactive writing: How language and literacy come together, K–2.* Portsmouth, NH: Heinemann.

National Association for the Education of Young Children and the International Reading Association. *Learning to read and write: Developmentally appropriate practices for young children.* Joint Position Statement.

National Council of Teachers of Mathematics & the National Association for the Education of Young Children. *Position statement on early childhood mathematics.* Washington, DC: Author.

Nielsen, D. M. (2002). *Preschool multiple intelligences.* Grand Rapids, MI: McGraw-Hill Children's Publishing

Ogle, D. (1986). K-W-L: A teaching model that develops active reading expository text. *Reading Teacher,* pp. 564–574.

Pianta, R. C., & Kraft-Sayre, M. (2003). *Successful kindergarten transition: Your guide to connecting children, families and schools.* Washington, DC: National Association for the Education of Young Children.

Raines, S., & Canady, R. (1989). *Story stretchers.* Beltsville, MD: Gryphon House.

Shore, R. (1997). *Rethinking the brain: New insights into early development.* New York: Families and Work Institute.

Strickland, D. S., & Schickedanz, J. A. (2005). *Learning about print in preschool: Working with letters, words, and beginning links with phonemic awareness.* Newark, DE: International Reading Association.

Warner, L., & Lynch, S. A. (2004). *Preschool classroom management: 150 teacher-tested techniques.* Beltsville, MD: Gryphon House.

Wolfe, P., & Nevills, P. (2004). *Building the reading brain, preK–3.* Thousand Oaks, CA: Corwin Press.

Index

CORWIN PRESS